# Inclusive Language in the Church

NANCY A. HARDESTY

*Foreword by Patrick D. Miller, Jr.*

John Knox Press
ATLANTA

**Library of Congress Cataloging-in-Publication Data**

Hardesty, Nancy.
    Inclusive language in the Church.

    Bibliography: p.
    Includes index.
    1. Language question in the church.  I. Title.
BR115.L25H37  1987      201'.4      86-46036
ISBN 0-8042-1686-X

© copyright John Knox Press 1987
10 9 8 7 6 5 4 3 2 1
Printed in the United States of America
John Knox Press
Atlanta, Georgia 30365

# *Foreword*

*P*ractical aids are not often written with passion. Vigorous critiques of current practice do not often give much help about how to change. The great merit of Nancy Hardesty's treatment of gender-oriented language is that it weds passion and practice, polemic and concrete alternatives, criticism and understanding. She joins many others in calling into fundamental question the noninclusive, gender-oriented language of the church, its Scriptures, and its tradition. This is not a light matter or a passing fad. It has to do with the most basic matters of faith and with the very possibility of Christian community. Reorientation of the way we think about ourselves and about God is not a matter for debate or an item on the theological agenda. It is for Hardesty a necessity for our life together and a matter of faithfulness to God. In that, she is correct, and the actual practice of persons and groups in the church suggests that hers is a word that needs to be said again and again.

Simple critique, even if strongly articulated, is not, however, Hardesty's primary goal in these pages. What she really offers is a kind of handbook, one that not only helps persons see the problems of our gender-shaped language—and the difficulties in overcoming that problem—but suggests many ways that change can be brought about. Her suggestions are concrete and eminently practical. They are radical in the sense of going to the roots of our faith but not in the sense of undercutting those roots or setting forth strange and unacceptable alternatives. In fact, many of her suggestions about how we can reshape both our language and our conceptuality are quite feasible and helpful. Counsels of despair, to wit that it is impractical, if not impossible, to speak of God without using masculine language or that the Bible is a historical document out of a male-oriented, patriarchal society that irrevocably stamps its language on communication, are thrust aside in favor of concrete suggestions about inclusive modes of theological speech and translation that, if followed, can produce better theologians and translators, even if they cannot solve all our problems.

For those who do not quite see the point about language, Hardesty gives sight, sometimes by logical reasoning or illustrations from past and present, sometimes by shaking the reader hard enough to bring the matter into focus. For those who know that our language matters and has to change, she shows the way and is a reliable guide. The end result is a resource that many individuals and groups within the church will find a positive help on a difficult but necessary journey.

Patrick D. Miller, Jr.
Princeton Theological Seminary

# Contents

*To*
*Melvin Lorentzen*
*who taught me how to write and so much more*

# Introduction

$M$any people consider the issue of inclusive language trivial or cosmetic, yet it goes to the very heart of the gospel.

"It just doesn't bother me!" That is the initial reaction of most people, women and men. Yet the heated, sometimes almost violent, discussion the issue has evoked makes one suspicious of that claim. And once the problem has been named, we become increasingly aware of it. Women particularly begin to realize the subconscious translation process that has been going on in our heads for years. Every time we have heard the words *man* or *men*, we have mentally calculated whether or not we are included.

For example, during the announcements at church we hear, "Men of the church are invited to a prayer breakfast next Saturday morning." Women rather quickly figure out that they are not invited. On the other hand, we hear the minister declare, "Rise up, O men of God, renew your commitment to God." This time women are not so sure whether or not they are invited. Is this a Father's Day sermon? Or is the minister simply paraphrasing the hymn? And does the hymn include women?

Once the issue has been raised, we become increasingly sensitized. The translation process becomes a conscious one. We become more and more aware of how often public speakers, ministers, writers use male words. The water torture begins. Like an incessant dripping on the head, the words come: *man, men, he, his, him, father, son, brethren, brotherhood.* Instead of joining in the intercession, one begins to count the times the pastor uses "Father" in a prayer. One begins to lose the points of sermons while fuming over statements like "Christ died for all men" and "God in Christ became man." The pain and anger become excruciating.

Rage mounts until one boils over or blows up. All of the pain and wrath pour out on whoever happens to be present. Rather than understanding the problem, the recipient of the anger usually just concludes that the assailant is crazy. This experience has led some to conclude that inclusive language is just an issue with the lunatic fringe of the women's movement. Actually it is an issue with every person, man or woman, whose consciousness has been raised concerning justice and equity for all people. One either walks out and never returns, as so many have, or one numbs out, becoming deaf to most of the message.

Even those of us who want to be sensitive toward others in the language we use sometimes have trouble getting our act together. In our heads we believe that inclusive language is right, and sometimes we are even willing to say so with our mouths—if we think speaking up will not bring down too much flak on us. Yet we may still not be inclusive in our guts; and our actions, our unconscious reactions, will reveal our inner unwillingness to let go of our prejudices.

When the issue of inclusive language first came to the fore, many people thought they could avoid it, trivialize and neutralize it with ridicule. I remember raising the issue more than a decade ago and having a well-known evangelical theologian ask me if I would prefer his saying "Awomen" at the end of his prayers instead of "Amen." Another wag suggested that perhaps we should sing "hers" instead of "hymns." (We evangelicals are seldom noted for a creative sense of humor!) In the public press columnists talked of changing manager to womanager, ignoring the fact that the root of the word manager is the Latin *manus* or hand, not the Old English and German *mann*. As these examples show, the subject does not generate much real humor.

Although educational textbook publishers were able quietly to make their books more inclusive, not only of girls and women but also of various ethnic groups, when inclusive language started to become a reality in the church, the confrontation turned ugly. The release of the National Council of Churches' *Inclusive Language Lectionary* and news of a proposal to review the Revised Standard Version of the Bible drew cries of outrage. The mere announcement of the projects drew more than ten thousand angry letters. The language of the responses was revealing. *Time* magazine (8 December 1980) headlined the story "Unmanning the Holy Bible: The sexual-textual revolution comes to Scripture," and the article spoke about "neutered wording." A story of 24 October 1983 alluded to a "de-sexed version of the Bible," improved to "degendered language" in the 29 October 1984 issue. The editors backslid, however, in the 3 December 1984 issue, headlining a letter to the editor, "Neutering the Bible."

Predictably more hostile was the response of the editors of *Christianity Today*. They took their basic stand in 1976 with an editorial bluntly titled: "He Meant What He Said: 'Him, His, He.'" They declared: "Of course the Bible gives offense. It was intended to do that." The editors continued to betray their bias by titling factual news reports on the *Inclusive Language Lectionary*, "God Our Father *and* Mother? A bisexual nightmare from the National Council of Churches" (11 November 1983) and "NCC's Bisexual Lectionary Brings More Problems" (16 December 1983). Presumably from these headlines one should assume that the Bible in the original autographs was "monosexual" and male. When a scholar submitted an article with the neutral title "The Bible and the English Language," *Christianity Today*'s editors heavily edited it to their own bias and printed it under the inflammatory title, "Toward a Neutered Bible: Making God S/He" (18 February 1983).

Conservative newspaper columnist James J. Kilpatrick revealed male fears more directly in his 23 October 1983 column when he denounced "the latest effort to castrate the Holy Bible." Declared Kilpatrick, "The National Council of Churches is out to take the sex out of Scripture." To my knowledge, no one has proposed eliminating Genesis or Song of Solomon from the canon. The use of inclusive language will not eliminate anything from Scripture or add anything substantial to it. It will simply communicate more clearly that the Bible's message is for all people, not just for men. But Kilpatrick's remarks illustrate the confusion and anxiety which many people experience around this subject.

Gender in language should not be confused with personal expressions of sexuality. Gender refers simply to male and female. Persons are assigned to either the male gender or the female gender. In some languages, such as Hebrew, Greek, Latin, French, Spanish, and German, all nouns, even those for inanimate objects and concepts, are assigned a gender: masculine, feminine, or neuter. All adjectives and pronouns referring to a given noun must have the corresponding gender ending. The gender of a noun has very little to do with the meaning of the noun—and the grammatical gender of a certain noun varies from language to language. In English we do not have gender endings on nouns, nor do we make adjectives agree with nouns in gender. We do use gender pronouns (*he*, *she*, and *it*), but normally we use *it* for everything other than persons or animals whose gender we know.

Sexuality is another subject entirely. Sexuality has to do with the energy we experience in relating to other people. It is a complex interaction of our physiological, psychological, sociological, and spiritual experiences. It is based on our biological differences as men and women, and it goes far beyond that, even though we often speak of it primarily in terms of genital definitions. The subject of sexuality gets injected into discussions of inclusive language because (1) the language issue has

4

been historically raised by women, (2) women have been negatively identified with sexuality in Western Christian culture, and (3) sexuality has been condemned as having nothing to do with spirituality. The ideal in the Christian tradition has historically (not biblically) been identified with the male, the rational, the transcendent, and the spiritual. The female, the emotional, the natural, and the sexual have been defined as polar opposites and condemned as sinful or at least suspect (for a fuller discussion see Dody H. Donnelly, *Radical Love*). Thus inclusive religious language strikes a raw nerve with some. Obviously it is neither a trivial nor cosmetic issue. Indeed it raises central theological questions.

Is there such a thing as "God's male gender" as the editors of *Christianity Today* made one writer say? Did God in Christ become man or human? Was Jesus, in the words of another *Christianity Today* article, "a man's man"? To use Rosemary Radford Ruether's question, "Can a male savior save women?" (*Sexism and God-Talk*, p. 116). Indeed if, as some theologians and a number of laypeople have asserted in the wake of the NCC's *Inclusive Language Lectionary*, "Christianity is a sexist religion," then do women have any place in it at all? In essence, the matter of inclusive language raises the question of the inclusiveness of the gospel.

Jonah was so appalled at the thought that God was "a gracious God and merciful, slow to anger, and abounding in steadfast love,"that he wanted to die (Jonah 4:2–3). He was enraged at the thought that God's love extended not only to the nation Israel but also to the Ninevites. Jesus' disciples "marveled" (John 4:27) that he talked with the woman of Samaria. Likewise many today are appalled and enraged when God's steadfast love is extended to women as well as men, when one asserts that women as well as men are included in the language of Scripture, that God even loves those of other denominations, other nations, other colors, and other religions than ours!

First Corinthians 6:9 does begin, "Do you not know that the unrighteous will not inherit the kingdom of God?" It concludes (vs. 11), "And such were some of you [indeed, such were all of us!]. But you were washed, you were sanctified, you were justified in the name of the Lord Jesus Christ and in the Spirit of our God." As Jesus himself said to those religious leaders who criticized him for eating with tax collectors and sinners, "I came not to call the righteous, but sinners" (Matt. 9:13; Mark 2:17; cf. Luke 5:32). Quoting the prophet Isaiah, Paul declared in Romans 3:10, "None is righteous, no, not one." Paul continues, "Since all have sinned and fall short of the glory of God, they are justified by [divine] grace as a gift, through the redemption which is in Christ Jesus" (vss. 23–24). Paul was certainly proud of his own heritage. He said he was "circumcised on the eighth day, of the people of Israel, of the tribe of Benjamin, a Hebrew born of Hebrews; as to the law a Pharisee . . ." (Phil. 3:5). But the gospel compelled him to say, "Then what becomes of our boasting? . . . Or is God the God of Jews only? Is [God] not the God of Gentiles also? Yes, of Gentiles also, since God is one" (Rom. 3:27, 29–30).

Peter was given the same message in a vision of a sheet dropped from heaven containing "all kinds of animals and reptiles and birds of the air" (Acts 10:12). The voice of God said, "Rise, Peter; kill and eat." Peter, the conscientious Jew, replied, "No, Lord; for I have never eaten anything that is common or unclean." God had to tell him three times, "What God has cleansed, you must not call common" (vs. 15), but Peter finally got the point. When he heard the call from the Roman Cornelius, he responded immediately and declared, "Truly I perceive that God shows no partiality, but in every nation any one who fears [the Lord] and does what is right is acceptable to [God]" (vss. 34–35).

As Paul declared in Galatians 3:28, "There is neither Jew nor Greek, there is neither slave nor free, there is neither male nor female; for you are all one in Christ Jesus." Inclusive language is simply a concrete expression of what we say we believe theologically: that all human beings are made in God's image, that salavation is free to all through the work of Christ on the cross, that in Christ all Christians are one body, one family.

**DISCUSSION:**

1. Draw a spectrum on the chalkboard or a piece of newsprint. Label the points along the way with positions such as "adamantly opposed to inclusive language," "moderately opposed," "don't like the fuss over it," "don't care one way or the other," "don't know what the fuss is all about," "it bothers me a little bit," "noninclusive language bugs me a lot!" "if the language used around here doesn't improve, I'm leaving!" When people arrive for the first discussion of this topic, have them make some mark designating where they are on that spectrum.

2. What is your initial reaction to the topic? What reactions have you heard from others about it?

3. How do you feel when someone says that "God is no respecter of persons," that "God shows no partiality"? Discuss Jonah's and Peter's reactions. How do you think they felt? What feelings of theirs do you share?

# I. The Whole Word

*T*hrough nature, through history, through the Bible, through the church, and most of all through the Word, Christ Jesus, God has been trying and continues to try to communicate with us.

Genesis 1:27 tells us that God created us, male and female, in God's own image. That very creation was the result of a discussion within the Godhead because verse 26 tells us that "then God said, 'Let us make [humanity] in our image, after our likeness.'" Immediately following our creation, God commanded us, "Be fruitful and multiply, and fill the earth and subdue it; and have dominion . . ." (vs. 28). God communicated to us our mission as a human race.

In the original creation, the Garden of Eden, God walked on the earth and talked with Adam and Eve face to face. Even after they disobeyed God and hid their faces, God continued to come—to Abraham and Sarah in human form, to Jacob as an angel, to Moses in the burning bush, to the children of Israel in a loud voice out of the thunder and lightning and clouds at Mount Sinai. God appeared and spoke to them.

Finally God took historical human form in Jesus the

Christ, Jesus the One anointed by God. Born of a woman, he ate and slept, walked the earth, healed the sick, and tried to teach those who would learn what God is like. Crucified, buried, and resurrected, Jesus Christ returned to the Godhead, baptizing those who would follow with the spirit, God living in us and continuing to speak to us and through us to the world.

Why has God gone to all of this trouble to communicate with us as human beings who have persisted in turning deaf ears and blind eyes? God loves us, totally, without reservation. God loves us, every one of us. Although we have in sin disfigured ourselves and each other, God continues to love us, to offer us healing and wholeness. Christ died for our salvation, our wholeness, our health, our *shalom*. The words are all related. The English word *salvation* is derived from Latin words meaning health and help, and from Greek words meaning cure, redemption, and rescue. The Hebrew word *shalom* means completeness, well-being, wholeness, health.

Both Judaism and Christianity teach that true religious faith is not a matter of belief in an orthodox creed but a vital relationship with the Living God. As the Gospel of John says, "the Word became flesh and dwelt among us, full of grace and truth" (1:14). The Samaritan woman at the well encountered the Living Water. Her immediate response was to share her discovery with her neighbors, who came and heard for themselves. In the end, they said, "It is no longer because of your words that we believe, for we have heard for ourselves, and we know that this is indeed the Savior of the world" (John 4:42).

## WORDS AND THE WORD

The words of Scripture, our words of witness, are always vehicles for communication. They are not divine in themselves but earthly tools with which we point to God. Scripture, inspired by God, is the authoritative word of God, but it is not God. It is one of many attempts made by God to communicate with us. No single word or group of words can ever capture God's essence. Each word or even group of words speaking of

God is still but one facet on a mirrored ball, reflecting but one ray of God's light.

God is beyond our every telling. As the Almighty reminded the prophet Isaiah,

> For my thoughts are not your thoughts,
>     neither are your ways my ways, says the LORD.
> For as the heavens are higher than the earth,
>     so are my ways higher than your ways
>     and my thoughts than your thoughts. (55:8–9)

We speak of God only by analogy. We use human words to try to explain something about God by comparing the divine with the human, by comparing that which is beyond all knowing with that which we know. Obviously our words are always limited, partial, approximate, and inadequate, and yet they are all we have to describe an experience of the Ineffable, that which is beyond adequate description. As Rosemary Radford Ruether reminds us, most historical world religions modeled their concepts of God after the ruling classes in their societies (*Sexism and God-Talk*, pp. 66, 69). As theologian Mary Daly declares in *Beyond God the Father*, "If God is male, then the male is God" (p. 19). Anne Wilson Schaef, in *Women's Reality*, speaks at length of "White Male Reality." The bottom line in that reality is that human beings can be God, which she reminds us has always been and still is the ultimate idolatry. It is part of our addictive system in which we believe that we mortals can control everything.

Thus we persist in speaking of God in male terms despite the second commandment's prohibition of making images and likenesses of the Deity (Exod. 20:4) and God's express statement in Hosea 11:9:

> I am God and not man [*'ish*, male],
>     the Holy One in your midst.

Nevertheless, God continues to communicate with us. Indeed that is precisely why God communicates with us in so many different ways—through the order and beauty of nature, the written word in Scripture; the spoken word of teaching, preaching, and counseling; the physical sacraments of water in baptism, bread and wine in communion, oil in anointing; the touch of lovers, family, and friends; the Living Word heard in prayer, meditation, and adoration. The Word is found in many different words, many of them nonverbal.

## DISCERNING THE WORD

Each medium, each type of word in the Living Word, has its own way of communicating. In order to understand each most fully, we must understand the rules for interpreting it. For example, much of the Bible is historical narrative, stories about the lives of various people who encountered God. The narrative allows us to stand beside these people and learn from them what they learned about God. Hannah explains to us as she explained to Eli, "I am the woman who was standing here in your presence, praying to the LORD. For this child I prayed; and the LORD has granted me my petition which I made" (1 Sam. 1:26–27). We learn with her that God graciously answers our petitions. In historical narratives either the people in the stories or the writers often tell us rather directly their point.

Many other types of writing in Scripture are not so explicit. How are we to understand such metaphors as "our God is a consuming fire" (Heb. 12:29)? The context suggests that God is one who responds to our sincere worship by accepting the offerings which we present, just as God sent down holy fire to consume Elijah's water-soaked offering in 1 Kings 18.

Jesus taught us about God through parables. Again we must learn to interpret them. We must discern the particular point being made. For example, we conclude from the story about the widow and the unrighteous judge in Luke 18 not that God is mean-spirited but rather that God will indeed answer our prayers if we, like the widow, persist in asking.

We all know that poetry is not to be taken literally—to say that "the LORD is my shepherd" does not mean that I am a four-footed woolly animal—yet many have received great comfort from Psalm 23. We realize that it speaks of God's love, care, and concern for us even in our ignorance and helplessness, even when we are "beastly."

Although the essence of the sacraments is mystery, Paul told us that "all of us who have been baptized into Christ Jesus were baptized into his death. We were buried therefore with him by baptism into death, so that as Christ was raised from the dead by the glory of the Father, we too might walk in newness of life" (Rom. 6:3–4). In Holy Communion we partake of the body and blood of Christ, are nourished and healed by it. *How* is mystery.

Nature also reveals God to us. We marvel at the vastness of interstellar space, at the intricacies of DNA, at the miracle of a newborn kitten, at the intensity of a hurricane. Our awed response is often just, "How great thou art!"

When we begin to think about it, we become aware of myriad ways in which God communicates with us in Scripture and beyond it. We become aware that we generally interpret what we believe God is saying according to the constraints of the media in which we find the message.

## THE GOOD NEWS

The essence of that message is that God loves every human being and seeks to offer us salvation. If that is true, then our explanations of the gospel and our proclamations of the good news must reflect that fact. All of our language must be inclusive. It must reflect the fact that all human beings—male and female, Black and white, yellow, brown, and red, rich and poor, gay and straight, old and young, educated and illiterate, healthy and infirm—all are made in God's image, loved by God, and candidates for salvation. Flannery O'Connor makes this point in a short story titled "A Temple of the Holy Ghost." She tells of a hermaphrodite in a carnival side show who tells those who come to view this "freak": "God made me thisaway and if you laugh He may strike you the same way." As the child in the story ponders this event, she imagines the hermaphrodite preaching to the onlookers:

"Raise yourself up. A temple of the Holy Ghost. You!
You are God's temple, don't you know? Don't you know?
God's Spirit has a dwelling in you, don't you know? . . .
    "If anybody desecrates the temple of God, God will
bring him to ruin and if you laugh, He may strike you
thisaway. A temple of God is a holy thing. Amen. Amen."

To speak only to the wealthy, the healthy, or the wise is
to distort the gospel. It is to say that God is captive of one camp
or another. It is to declare that God is indeed a respecter of persons, that God's love is selective and partial rather than unconditional and universal. To choose to use only a few of the
images of God offered to us in Scripture is to offer only a frag-
ment of the gospel.

Many Christians readily condemn various sects and cults
for making some minor biblical point or some distorted doctrine
into their central creed, yet we do much the same thing ourselves when we refuse to accept and use the riches of God's
word. We too would tear one or two pages from our Bibles and
offer it as the totality of God's word. While the pages we choose
may be sweet and nourishing to us, these same pages may be
bitter and sickening to others. The Bible contains both milk and
meat. We must offer the whole book, the entire meal.

Roman Catholic theologian Gregory Baum, in a book
titled *Man Becoming*, says:

> To believe that God is Father is to become aware of oneself not
> as stranger, not as an outsider or an alienated person, but as a
> son who belongs or a person appointed to a marvelous destiny,
> which he shares with the whole community. To believe that
> God is Father means to be able to say "we" in regard to all
> men. (p. 195)

Such a statement is incredibly alienating to most women. We
become daughters who do not belong, persons without
destiny, outside the community. To believe in such a God is
sometimes to be unable to say "we" at all. No wonder a little
girl named Sylvia once wrote, "Dear God, Are boys better than
girls? I know you are one but try to be fair" (*Children's Letters to
God*). Civil rights activist and Episcopal priest Pauli Murray has

put it another way. She notes that declaring to a congregation of women and men that we worship the God of Abraham, Isaac, and Jacob is equivalent to speaking of the "God of white people" to a Black congregation ("The Holy Spirit and God Language," p. 8).

## INCLUSIVE LANGUAGE

Many people think that pleas for nonsexist language are requests for the elimination of certain traditional and beloved forms of language. Indeed some feminists have presented the matter in a negative way, suggesting at least a moratorium on the use of certain male-identified words. What this book suggests is that we expand and enrich our vocabularies rather than further restricting them. Indeed we have often been as children limited to the vocabulary of our first-grade primer rather than as adults who have the wealth of a dictionary before us.

The more ways in which we learn to understand God and to speak of God, the more deeply we will know God. Truly inclusive language will vastly expand our own theological knowledge of God and the divine workings in our lives. It will enrich the contemplation and adoration of our devotional lives. Russian Orthodox Metropolitan Anthony Bloom advises in his helpful little book *Beginning to Pray*,

> Unless we can find the right name for God, we have no free, real, joyful, open access to [God]. As long as we have to call God by general terms like "The Almighty," "The Lord God," as long as we have got to put "the" before the word to make it anonymous, to make it a generic term, we cannot use it as a personal name. (p. 67)

He goes on to point out how David was moved to exclaim in the Psalms, "O, you, my joy!" (see Psalm 43:4). The mystics spoke of God in many ways. Mechthild of Magdeburg spoke of the Flowing Light of the Godhead; Richard Rolle described God as Burning Love (*Incendium Amoris*). The mystics spoke of God as the Absolute, the Abyss, the Alone, the Divine Dark; they also experienced God most intimately as a feeling of warmth within, the sound of celestial music, the smell of sweet incense, the presence of transcendent light, the rush of wind. And thus Augustine called God "the One"; Plotinus, "the Supplier of True Life"; Dante, "Eternal Light"; and Catherine of Genoa, "Pure Love" (see Underhill, *Mysticism,* p. 331).

On a human level, an effort to use more inclusive language makes us aware not only of our sexism, but also of our racism, elitism, nationalism, classism, ageism, homophobia, and all our other prejudices. The Golden Rule, which Christ gave us in Matthew 7:12 and Luke 6:31, suggests that we should "do unto others as we would have them do unto us." Most of us are very sensitive to words which we feel denigrate us—slurs on our ethnic heritage or comments about our anatomy or remarks about our personality traits. For example, I bristle at the old cliché about redheads having bad tempers, and I am not amused by comic Joan Rivers' "fat" jokes. Yet often we are quite insensitive to those words which similarly hurt others. An emphasis on inclusive language helps us truly to be good neighbors, sensitive members of the human family, parts of one body—able to suffer and rejoice together (1 Cor. 12:26).

Inclusive language will also empower our evangelism. The Great Physician offers medicine for the healing of the world's hurts. By using noninclusive language we have been like pharmacists dispensing aspirin to everyone. For some patients it may have been helpful, but for others it has been useless and sometimes even harmful. Inclusive language offers God the opportunity to prescribe the precise medicine needed by each suffering soul.

Thus, using inclusive language is not merely a matter of taste or literary sophistication but a matter of faithfulness to God and to our moral responsibility for our neighbors. As the report on "Language About God" to the former Presbyterian Church in the United States says, "Language about God commonly used only a decade ago has now become for many an impediment to communication, community, and to faith itself" (p.7). To speak accurately of God and lovingly to our neighbor requires the use of inclusive language. Anything less is a rejection of God's revelation of God's selfhood and a withholding of God's gift to the needy, food for the hungry, and cure for the sick.

On a religious level some fear that an emphasis on inclusive language is an attempt to rewrite the Bible. Indeed, as we will see in the following chapters, our goal is rather to appreciate and use the riches of Scripture and Christian tradition as well as religious experience.

And why should we fear that in broadening our language some of us will use the wrong words, unbiblical words? Worship, prayer, devotion, even theological discussion are not matters of the correct magical incantation. God is here whether the rite is right or wrong. Calling on God is not a long distance telephone call in which the matter of one wrong digit could connect us with Hong Kong. We do not even have to know the right area code or zip code to contact God! God is with us always (Matt. 28:20). God knows our hearts and the Spirit stands ready to translate even our sighs and groans (Rom. 8:26–27). All we need to do is turn to God and open ourselves to the Divine Presence.

On a more profane level many argue that inclusive language "is too much work just to please a few fanatics." Actually the issue is relevant to every person, male and female, but even if only one person were to be offended, is not the value of that soul worth it? Did not Jesus tell three parables in a row—the Lost Sheep, the Lost Coin, and the Prodigal Son (Luke 15)—to illustrate God's seeking out that one lost soul?

Indeed the skills of good writing and persuasive speaking do take work. Using inclusive language is no easier nor more difficult than being grammatically correct or theologically precise. All are the tasks of those of us who seek to follow the scriptural injunction to "do your best to present yourself to God as one approved, a work[er] who has no need to be ashamed, rightly handling the word of truth" (2 Tim. 2:15).

God calls us to be as inclusive in our language as in our love. Jesus said: "If you love those who love you, what credit is that to you? For even sinners love those who love them" (Luke 6:32). One might paraphrase the question: "If you communicate with those who communicate with you, what credit is that to you? For even sinners speak to each other." Our goal as Christians should be to communicate the gospel to all and to communicate all of the gospel. This is our task.

## DISCUSSION:

1. Share the ways in which God communicates with you. Think about the times when you have felt closest to God or when you have felt that God spoke directly to you about something.

2. How do you think we can decide when a message is really from God and when we are simply listening to the voice of our culture or tradition or some worldly authority or prejudice or our own fears? Think of some historical examples where the church may have listened to the wrong voices.

3. Sometimes we confuse the medium with the message. For example, some people worship nature rather than the Creator. Can you think of other examples? How can we avoid idolatry?

4. Do you really believe that all people are included in God's love? All of us grew up with hosts of prejudices about other people. What prejudicial messages did you get from your parents, your schoolmates, maybe even your church? Have your experiences since then changed any of those prejudices? Do you still need to work to rid yourself of some prejudices?

5. What do you think is the essence of the good news, the gospel? Each of us phrases it in our own way, the way that is most meaningful to us. Write what the gospel is for you in a sentence or a short paragraph. Share these with the group.

6. Beyond those given, can you think of other reasons why attention to inclusive language is important?

# II. God the Revealer

$G$od's goal in human history is self-revelation. God created human beings to be in communication with the divine. In the beginning, the Lord God walked in the garden in the cool of the day, seeking conversation with the creatures newly created. Even after they had sinned and had been expelled from the garden, God continued to appear—to Abraham and Sarah under the oak of Mamre, to Hagar in the wilderness, to Moses in the burning bush on the back side of the desert, to the people of Israel at Mount Sinai, to Elijah in the cave on Mount Horeb, to Daniel in the lion's den, to Peter, James, and John on the Mount of Transfiguration, to Mary Magdalene at the tomb, to Paul on the road to Damascus, to John on the Isle of Patmos. God continually tried to communicate through the judges, the prophets, the apostles, the Scriptures, the church.

As A. W. Tozer puts it in *The Pursuit of God*: "self-expression is inherent in the Godhead." God is "forever seeking to speak . . . to . . . creation." Indeed God is by "nature continuously articulate" (p. 73). The Creator wants us creatures to know and love the One who created us. When one avenue of communication is blocked or resisted, God tries another—and another.

God's nature is indeed beyond human conception, certainly beyond description in human language. Theologians say that all language about God is analogous, which means that we are always describing God in human terms. We anthropomorphize God—we speak of God in human terms like father or mother or judge—and we anthropopathize God—we describe God as having human emotions like love, anger, sadness. Almost everything we say about God is in the language of metaphor. Rather than limiting our knowledge of God to concrete propositions, metaphor opens our minds and hearts to an ever-expanding understanding of God. To quote A. W. Tozer again, "It will be a great moment for some of us when we begin to believe that God's promise of self-revelation is literally true: that [the Lord] promised much, but promised no more than [God] intends to fulfill"(p.65).

## *NAMING GOD*

In the Hebrew Scriptures, God is most often designated by one of three words: *El, Elohim,* or *Yahweh.*

*El* is the basic, generic word meaning God in the Semitic languages. It can refer to any god, true or false, or any person or object treated as a god. Thus, to make it more specific, writers often preceded it with a defining adjective or verb. For example, in Deuteronomy 5:9 we read, "I the LORD [*Yahweh*] your God [*Elohim*] am a jealous God [*El*]." *El* is the designation commonly used in the E source, referred to as the Elohist history. The Canaanites used the term as a proper name for their high God whose son was Ba'al.

*Elohim,* which is a plural form, is often treated as a singular form meaning the one supreme deity. In English translations, it too is usually rendered God. It is an abstract noun referring to the character of deity, though in Scripture it is frequently used in ways suggesting a proper noun. Interestingly, it is the designation for God used throughout Genesis 1, including verse 27 which declares we were made in the image of God, male and female. *Eloah*, the singular form, is used forty-two times in Job, plus fifteen times elsewhere (see Deut. 32:15, 18; Neh. 9:17; Pss. 18:31; 50:22; 114:7; 139:19; Prov. 30:5; Isa. 44:8). Some people interpret the use of the plural *Elohim* as a carry-over from its use in polytheism; others view it as a prefiguring of the revelation of the Trinity.

The original Hebrew word *YHWH*, called the tetragrammaton because it has four letters, was considered so awesome and holy that after the Exile it was not even vocalized by pious Jewish people. When Jews read the Torah in the Temple or synagogue, they substituted the word *Adonai*, which means *my Lord*. In modern times the vowels from this word were erroneously combined with *YHWH* to get *Jehovah*. The spelling *Yahweh* comes from the transliteration of the name into Greek in early Christian times, though it was probably not vocalized in this form in ancient times. While the contemporary Jerusalem Bible uses "Yahweh," most versions of the Bible continue the Jewish tradition of substituting LORD, using large and small capital letters to distinguish it from other instances when they are simply translating *Adonai* as Lord (in which case they use a capital letter and then lower-case letters). In some ways this common practice sets a precedent for this book's suggestion that a name of God be substituted for masculine pronouns in reading and transcribing Scripture, since the version of the Bible we are reading probably already uses a substitution rather than a literal translation of references to God.

*Yahweh* is a proper name for Israel's God, though many scholars would insist it is not meant to be a name in the Hebrew sense of summing up the named one's essence, but is simply another description. It is, paradoxically, an ineffable name. It is found as one of the identifying marks of the J source (J being used instead of Y in German and German scholars being the first to outline the documentary hypothesis).

By this designation, God is introduced to Israel. In reply to Moses' question concerning the identification of the deity who is commissioning him, God said, "Say this to the people of Israel, 'The LORD [*Yahweh*], the God [*Elohim*] of your fathers, the

God of Abraham, the God of Isaac, and the God of Jacob, has sent me to you': this is my name for ever, and thus I am to be remembered throughout all generations" (Exod. 3:15). God's apparently enigmatic answer, translated "I AM WHO I AM" in English (vs. 14), is not a new name, but the underlying meaning of the name Moses already knew, *Yahweh*. Martin Buber translates it, "I will be as I will be." Others suggest it means "I cause to be what comes into existence."

Although many Christian scholars use the term *Yahweh* freely, others note that religious Jews find such usage sacrilegious and offensive. Thus the careful writer and speaker will want to limit its use. It should not be used casually as an alternative for "God."

These words are combined with each other and with other terms to provide a variety of ways to refer to the deity. For example, the second creation account in Genesis 2:4—3:24 uses a combination, *Yahweh Elohim*. Another divine title is *Yahweh Sebaot*, "the LORD of hosts, " which does not appear in the Pentateuch but is the title by which God was worshiped at Shiloh and is common in the prophets. For example, Jeremiah prefaces many of his prophecies with the authorization, "Thus says the LORD of hosts, the God of Israel" (Jer. 7:3, 21; 9:15; 16:9; 19:3, 15; 25:27; 27:4). In Genesis 21:33 Abraham, after making a covenant with Abimelech, planted a tamarisk tree in Beersheba and "called there on the name of the LORD, the Everlasting God [*Yahweh el olam*]."

*Yahweh* is also combined with other words to form descriptive names. The title *Yahweh-yirah* was a favorite of early Pentecostalists; it means "the LORD provides" (cf. Gen. 22:8, 14). *Yahweh-nissi* means "the LORD is my banner" (Exod. 17:15). Likewise *Yahweh-shalom* means "the LORD is peace" (Judg. 6:24). The Messiah is spoken of as *Yahweh-tsidkenu*, "the LORD is our righteousness" (Jer. 23:6, 33:16). Another precious image is God our healer, *Yahweh-rophi* (Exod. 15:26).

Deborah uses the combination *Yahweh elohe Yisrael*, "the LORD, the God of Israel" (Judg. 5:3). Isaiah's favorite way to speak of God seems to be *qedosh Yisrael*, "the Holy One of

Israel" (twenty-nine times, beginning in Isa. 1:4); it is also used by Jeremiah and in the Psalms. Similar are *abir Yisrael*, "the Mighty One of Israel," and *nesah Yisrael*, "the Strength of Israel" (1 Sam. 15:29, KJV) or "the Glory of Israel," (RSV).

Melchizedek, in his meeting with Abraham, blesses him in the name of *El Elyon*, "God Most High, maker of heaven and earth" (Gen. 14:19), whom Abraham acknowledges as his God as well (vs. 22). The Old Testament name Eliezer was taken from the term *El-ezer*, "God is my help," and Elijah means "My God is *Yahweh.*" *El-berith* is the God of Covenant (Judg. 9:46). Hagar in Genesis 16:13 "called the name of the LORD who spoke to her" in the wilderness *El Roi:* "Thou art a God of seeing." In symbol God is sometimes portrayed as an eye within a triangle (see the symbol on the back of a U.S. one-dollar bill).

## *EL SHADDAI*

One name which has generated considerable discussion is *El Shaddai* or simply *Shaddai*. It has also recently been used in several popular songs. It is usually translated Almighty God by King James scholars. Jerome and the women who translated the Vulgate understood it to mean omnipotent (*pantokrator*), while the rabbis' midrashic exegesis suggests it means self-sufficiency.

Most scholars today think that it was derived from the Akkadian word *shadu*, meaning mountain. Yahweh is often associated with such mountains as Sinai, Horeb, Zion, or Moriah. Nevertheless, the title probably came originally from the Amorites, who conceived their god as the one of the mountains. However, biblical scholar David Biale, in a provocative article in *History of Religions* suggests that it may be derived rather from the Old Akkadian *shadwi* meaning breast, *shad* in Hebrew ("The God with Breasts," p. 246). Obviously the two definitions need not be mutually exclusive! Biale notes that scholars have followed the lead of William F. Albright, who in 1935 decided that *shadu* meant mountain while acknowledging that its original meaning was probably breast.

All of these meanings may have beer
ancient history to biblical authors, who offe'
this particular title, as they sometimes do fr
associated with the priestly tradition, it is
thor of Job, usually considered to be the oldesɪ ᴠ
Testament. However, the name is particularly associatᴠ
fertility blessings. For example, in Genesis 49:25–26 Jacob prays
for his sons,

> by the God of your father who will help you,
>   by God Almighty [*El Shaddai*] who will bless you
>   with blessings of heaven above,
> blessings of the deep that couches beneath,
>   blessings of the breasts [*shadayim*] and of the womb
>   [*rahem*].
> The blessings of your father
>   are mighty beyond the blessings of the eternal mountains,
>   the bounties of the everlasting hills.

This interpretation does amplify the meaning of such passages
as Genesis 28:3 in which Isaac prays for Jacob, saying, "God Almighty [*El Shaddai*] bless you and make you fruitful and multiply you," a refrain associated with other occurrences of the title
in Genesis 17:1,5–6; 35:11; 43:14; 48:3–4 (see also Trible, p. 61).

God is portrayed as giving birth in several passages (cf.
Deut. 32:18; Isa. 49:15; 66:7–9). In Deuteronomy 32 God is por-
trayed in parallel fashion as father and mother. In verse 6
Moses asks,

> Is not he your father, who created you,
>   who made you and established you?

Later in verse 18 Moses rephrases the accusation in female
terms:

> You were unmindful of the Rock that begot [*bore*] you,
>   and you forgot the God who gave you birth.

(In Hebrew the word *yld*, here translated *begot*, can also mean
the natural act of bearing a child. Though the verb *hyl* in the
phrase "who gave you birth" can only refer to labor pains, the
Jerusalem Bible betrays masculine bias in translating the phrase

23

*"the God who fathered you!"*) In cursing Israel, Hosea 9:14
likewise asks:

> Give them, O LORD—
> what wilt thou give?
> Give them a miscarrying womb
> and dry breasts.

Yet Isaiah 49:15 promises:

> Can a woman forget her sucking child,
> that she should have no compassion on the son of her
> womb?
> Even these may forget,
> yet I will not forget you.

(The word *shaddai* may indeed be more directly related to the
Egyptian verb *shdi* meaning to suckle, according to Biale.)
   The image of God as mother is also found in Psalm 131:2,
where the psalmist says,

> ... I have calmed and quieted my soul,
> like a child quieted at its mother's breast;
> like a child that is quieted is my soul.

In Hosea 11:3–4 God says,

> Yet it was I who taught Ephraim to walk,
> I took them up in my arms;
> but they did not know that I healed them.
> I led them with cords of compassion,
> with the bands of love,
> and I became to them as one
> who eases the yoke on their jaws,
> and I bent down to them and fed them.

James L. Mays in his Old Testament Library commentary on
Hosea translates the second line, "I was to them like those
who lift a baby to their cheeks," a tender parental image.
   Phyllis Trible, in her book *God and the Rhetoric of Sexuality*,
traces the "Journey of a Metaphor" created by related Hebrew
words (pp. 31–59). Beginning with the noun *rehem*, which
means womb or uterus, she looks at the use of its cognates:
*rahamim*, the plural form meaning also the abstractions of com-

passion, mercy, and love; the verb *rhm*, meaning to show mercy, and the adjective *rahum*, meaning merciful. A second word for womb, *beten*, is often used in parallel. Trible begins by noting that in Scripture the wombs of women are controlled not by the women or by their husbands but by God, Yahweh (cf. Gen. 20:1–18; 29:31–35; 30:22; 1 Sam. 1:1–10; Jer. 1:5; Job 10:18–19; 31:13–15; see also 3:1–26).

In Psalm 22:9–10 God appears also to be a midwife:

> Yet thou art he who took me from the womb [*beten*];
>   thou didst keep me safe upon my mother's breasts.
> Upon thee was I cast from my birth,
>   and since my mother bore me thou hast been my God.

Trible translates the final lines more literally:

> Upon thee was I cast from the womb [*rehem*],
>   from the womb [*beten*] of my mother my God thou art.

In Isaiah God claims Israel,

> who have been borne by me from your birth [literally,
>   from the womb, *beten*],
> carried from the womb [*raham*] (46:3–4).

This metaphor is the context for the repeated description of God as merciful, *rahum*. The word in its adjectival form is used only for the Creator and never for creatures. Usually coupled with the word *gracious*, it is found throughout the Old Testament in all types of literature from all periods. "The LORD merciful and gracious" is found in a variety of settings (cf., e.g., Exod. 33:19; 34:6; Deut. 4:31; 2 Chron. 30:9; Neh. 9:17; Ps. 86:15; 103:8; 111:4; 112:4; 145:8; Joel 2:13; Jon. 4:2).

God also speaks of and is spoken of as *showing compassion*, again a form of the word for womb. In the fascinating poem in Jeremiah 31:15–22, which is filled with female images, God calls Ephraim, "my dear son. . . . my darling child" and then declares that "my womb trembles for him; I will truly show motherly-compassion [*rahem arahamennu*] upon him" (vs. 20, Trible's translation). Trible notes that the words she translates here "womb trembles" are literally *inner-parts tremble* (*hamu me' ay*), a phrase which is used in an erotic context in Song of Solomon 5:4 but elsewhere parallels the use of *womb* (cf. Gen. 25:23; Ps. 71:6; and Isa. 49:1) (p. 45).

On the other hand, God can withhold such compassion. Isaiah 27:11 warns the people that

> he who made them will not have compassion on them,
> he that formed them will show them no favor.

Similarly in Jeremiah 13:14 Yahweh warns, "I will not pity or spare or have compassion, that I should not destroy them." Other examples could be cited (cf. Isa. 9:17). Is this perhaps why *Shaddai* is the name of God that Naomi uses of the one who dealt bitterly with her, afflicted her, and brought calamity (Ruth 1:20–21)?

Moses combines a series of feminine images of God in his prayer to God concerning the rebellious children of Israel: "Did I conceive all this people? Did I bring them forth, that thou shouldst say to me, 'Carry them in your bosom, as a nurse carries the sucking child, to the land which thou didst swear to give their fathers?' "(Num. 11:12). Moses thus implies that God, not he, is the people's mother, midwife, and wet nurse.

Jesus spoke of being born again "of water and the Spirit" (John 3:5), of God giving us spiritual birth as our mothers gave us physical birth. And the image of God as nursing mother persisted in church history as well. Clement of Alexandria wrote that "to those infants who seek the Word, the Father's loving breasts supply milk." The Third Council of Toledo spoke of the Father's womb, *de utero patri*. Perhaps this echoes Psalm 103:13 which, in a rare Old Testament use of *Father*, speaks of God as a father who "pities" his children, again using cognates of *rehem*. Chrysostom, the great preacher, called God "Sister, Mother," and Anselm, who developed the philosophical ontological argument for God's existence, prayed to Jesus as Mother. In the fourteenth century Julian of Norwich also spoke of Jesus as the mother who gives us birth in the agonies of the cross and who nurses us at the breast in holy communion:

Our true Mother Jesus, he alone bears us for joy and for endless life, blessed may he be. So he carries us within him in love and travail, until the full time when he wanted to suffer the sharpest thorns and cruel pains that ever were or will be, and at the last he died. And when he had finished, and had borne us so for bliss, still all this could not satisfy his wonderful love. . . .

The mother can give her child to suck of her milk, but our precious Mother Jesus can feed us with himself, and does, most courteously and most tenderly, with the blessed sacrament, which is the precious food of true life . . . . (*Showings*, p. 298)

Thus the *Inclusive Language Lectionary* is within this tradition of both andropomorphic and gynomorphic images of God when it uses "Our Father [and Mother]" or "[Our Mother and] Father."

## IS GOD OUR FATHER?

One of the most problematic descriptions of God for feminists is Father. Though it appears less than ten times in the Old Testament and with frequency only in Matthew and John, many male theologians and pastors argue that this is the name Jesus used and taught us to use in prayer. Therefore they insist on using it in every prayer. The result is to project patriarchy into heaven, indeed into the Godhead, and thus to buttress the authority of earthly males—not only male parents but husbands over wives, clergymen over laity, male political leaders over women. One must ask: is this the thrust of biblical revelation?

A careful reading of the New Testament reveals quite the opposite. Some would insist that we call God Father on the basis of the historical fact that we affirm Jesus to be the son of the Virgin Mary and thus God is Jesus' "father." It always amazes me that precisely some of the most orthodox people argue in this manner. While asserting their staunch belief in the miracle of the virgin birth, they simultaneously debase it into just another pagan myth similar to Zeus' taking the form of a swan to copulate with the beautiful Leda. In attempting to "elevate" the stature of women in the Christian faith, one evangelical leader once declared that after all, God did not rape Mary but gave her a choice as to whether she would accept the pregnancy! His mental image is crystal clear: he does not believe in a truly virgin birth but in a male deity who at least on that occasion physically impregnated a willing human female. To truly assert that Jesus was the product of a virgin birth, as I believe he was, is to affirm a mystery, just as it is to say that Jesus was God Incarnate, fully God and fully human. To say that God was Jesus' physical father is as much heresy as to say that God was the source of Jesus' spirit and Mary was merely the source of his body. The church fought for centuries trying to articulate a faith which avoided such dualities, false divisions, and anthropomorphism.

Jesus, moreover, stressed that his real family was not his biological one, but rather "those who hear the word of God and keep it" (Luke 11:28). "Whoever does the will of God is my brother, and sister, and mother" (Mark 3:35). Indeed Jesus cut to the heart of patriarchy by declaring, "I have not come to bring peace, but a sword. For I have come to set a man [*anthropos*] against his father, and a daughter against her mother. . . . [The one] who loves father or mother more than me is not worthy of me" (Matt. 10:34–37) and, "If any one comes to me and does not hate [their] own father and mother and wife and children and brothers and sisters, yes, and even [their] own life, [they] cannot be my disciple" (Luke 14:26). The community of the kingdom, God's realm, are those who have "left house or brothers or sisters or mother or father or children or lands, for my sake and for the gospel." They will receive "a hundredfold now in this time, houses and brothers and sisters and mothers and children and lands, with persecutions, and in the age to come eternal life" (Mark 10:29–30).

Jesus declared that we should call no man father on earth precisely because we "have one Father, who is in heaven" (Matt. 23:9). This statement is preceded by the injunction, "You are not to be called rabbi, for you have one teacher, and you are all [brothers and sisters]" (vs. 8) and followed by the warning, "Neither be called masters, for you have one master, the

Christ" (vs. 10). Jesus' warning against Pharisaism ends, the one "who is greatest among you shall be your servant; whoever exalts [one]self will be humbled, and whoever humbles [one]self will be exalted"( vss. 11–12). In Mark 10:42–44 and Luke 22:24–27 Jesus reminds the disciples that "those who are supposed to rule over Gentiles lord it over them, and their great [ones] exercise authority over them. But it shall not be so among you; but whoever would be great among you must be your servant" (Mark 10:42–43). In Jesus' prayers, his address was always to the Father "in Heaven," clearly pointing to a unique relationship and designation, not to be confused with earthly relationships.

Thus using the designation of God as "Father" in order to legitimate patriarchy is to violate the third commandment, to take the Lord's name in vain. One must heed the warning given there: "the LORD will not hold [anyone] guiltless who takes [God's] name in vain" (Exod. 20:7).

Some people try to make a distinction between the way the term Father is used in such statements as "God is the Father" and statements in Scripture which say, "God is like a mother." In technical literary terms, the first is a metaphor, which makes a comparison between two things by saying that one *is* the other, and the second is a simile, which makes a comparison between two things by saying that one is *like* or *as* the other. Though the wording differs, the two figures of speech do the same thing—make comparisons, trying to illumine the first idea by comparing it with something else with which the reader or listener is presumably more familiar. The difference between metaphor and simile is grammatical; it is not semantic. The first is not intended to be a statement of being. It is a metaphor, not a theological proposition. "The boss is a bear" is seldom understood literally to mean that one works for a grizzly or a panda.

The concept of God as father may have been intended to personalize the Transcendent One, the Absolute, the Ancient of Days. We have extended the process to the point of trivialization. The Aramaic word *Abba* is mentioned only three times in the New Testament (Mark 14:36; Rom. 8:15 and Gal. 4:6). Sentimental burble about how Jesus habitually prayed to God as "Daddy" is tripe. Although the word was used by a child to its father, it was also frequently the respectful address of a student to a rabbi. It does, however, affirm a primary relationship of love and trust, certainly not a relationship of stark obedience based on fear, as some would portray the proper human response to Deity.

Yet the image of God as father can be a useful one. I personally found it troubling until one Sunday morning when I visited a church I used to attend in Chicago. I knew that God must be trying to tell me something when the minister announced that while he had previously skipped the term Father in his series of sermons on the Lord's Prayer, he was ready to preach about it that morning! Indeed his message remains with me every time I repeat the prayer.

He began by explaining that since God was Spirit and beyond gender distinctions, asserting that God was male was obviously not Jesus' intention in using the term. Instead the minister argued that in using the title and in giving us the prayer, Jesus was offering to us a legal and emotional relationship. We Episcopalians begin the "Our Father" prayer at holy communion after the priest's invitation, "And now, as our Savior Christ has taught us, we are bold to say. . . ." The minister made the point that only because Jesus Christ is our Savior do we have the audacity to affirm this intimate relationship to God and to ask for forgiveness and sustenance.

Feminist theologian Diane Tennis has written a provocative book on the subject: *Is God the Only Reliable Father?* She pleads that we continue to call God Father because God is a reliable father in an age when many fathers are absent or emotionally unavailable. She suggests that many women in particular resist any move to limit the use of language about God as father because they yearn to relate to a good father and are intensely angry at the failure of the fathers in their lives. Likewise men suffer from the absence of good fathering and feel guilt at their own inadequacy. Tennis feels that God offers a model of a father that is not remote, solitary, or self-sufficient, but rather involved, trustworthy, and emotionally available.

One final word must be said about images of God as parent in general. Sometimes all of us need the comfort and security, the unconditional love that the ideal parent gives. Thus the images of God as mother and father can be deeply meaningful. On the other hand, all of us also know the adolescent's need for independence, for a separate individual identity. We must also be very careful not to project our distorted, sexist family patterns onto God, patterns of oppression of husbands over wives, parents over children. In the New Testament's use of parent-child images, the focus is on relationship. We are one in the family of God. We are God's heirs. We can depend on God. But God has no interest in keeping us in perpetual dependency, always one down, or under parental authority. We are repeatedly encouraged to be childlike and yet to give up childish ways (see 1 Cor. 13:11), to not be children in our thinking but mature (1 Cor. 14:20), to "go on to maturity"(Heb. 6:1), to attain the full stature of adult Christ-likeness (Eph. 4:13).

For Christian leaders to affirm only the fatherhood of God can become just an attempt to buttress their own positions of authority, to identify their own masculinity with God's supposed masculinity, thus making themselves false gods. They not only falsify the image of God but violate the model of authority given us by Christ, who told the disciples they were to lead as he did, as one who serves.

## GOD AS ACTOR

Father and Mother are certainly not the only roles given in Scripture to describe God's nature and relationship to us. That we think of some of them in gender-related terms is often a reflection of occupational sex-role stereotyping in our contemporary culture. Indeed, contrary to most discussions of the topic, the majority of the language about God in Scripture is not gender-related.

In the beginning God was our Creator, our Maker. In Isaiah 44:24, God declares:

Thus says the LORD, your Redeemer,
  who formed you from the womb:

"I am the LORD, who made all things,
  who stretched out the heavens alone,
  who spread out the earth. . . ."

Jeremiah "went down to the potter's house" (ch. 18) to learn that God, like the potter, can create a vessel and also destroy and rework a marred vessel. Job 10:8–9 uses the same image:

Thy hands fashioned and made me;
  and now thou dost turn about and destroy me.
Remember that thou hast made me of clay;
  and wilt thou turn me to dust again?

Adelaide A. Pollard put the thought into a hymn:

Have Thine own way, Lord!
Have Thine own way!
Thou art the Potter;
I am the clay.
Mold me and make me
After thy will,
While I am waiting,
Yielded and still.

Jesus used a related image when he likened the kingdom or reign of God to a woman who puts yeast or leaven with flour to create bread (Matt. 13:33; Luke 13:20–21). God is the baker making the bread, the kingdom.

God's sovereignty is reflected in such images as king, ruler, judge. The Israelites begged for an earthly king to lead them; God would have preferred that they continue to rely on divine rule without earthly embodiment, perhaps because in their society ruling would be limited to males. The psalmist speaks of God as the "King of glory" (Ps. 24:7–10), a "great King above all gods" (Ps. 95:3). For king, the *Inclusive Language Lectionary* substitutes "ruler" or "monarch," substitutions that retain the point of the images without implying exclusively male referents.

When God ruled the people of Israel through the Judges, God chose Deborah as well as Gideon, Samson, and the rest. The Bible speaks of God as judge repeatedly. When God told Abraham that Sodom and Gommorah would be destroyed, Abraham appealed, "Shall not the Judge of all the earth do right?" (Gen. 18:25). Jesus even likens God to a rather nasty judge who eventually gives in to a woman's cries for justice just because she persists in pleading her case (Luke 18:1–7). In the Nicene Creed we affirm that Christ shall come again in glory to judge the living and the dead. Isaiah puts all three concepts together: "The LORD is our judge, the LORD is our ruler, the LORD is our king" (Isa. 33:22).

One of our most beloved images from both the Old and New Testaments is of God the Good Shepherd. Through the centuries, Psalm 23 has brought comfort to millions of dying and bereaved people, even those who have seen sheep only in pictures. Jesus in John 10 used the image of himself as the shepherd who protects and calls his own. Jesus used it again in one of his most famous parables concerning the shepherd who leaves ninety-nine sheep to look for the lost one (Matt. 18:10–14; Luke 15:4–7). Elizabeth Clephane turned the story into a poem "The Ninety and Nine," which Ira Sankey put hauntingly to music. Innumerable Christmas pageants have led us to think of shepherds as boys or men in bathrobes, but Rachel was a shepherd when Jacob first met and fell in love with her (Gen. 29:4–12). Thus *shepherd* need not be a gender-specific image.

In the parables Jesus also pictures God as a sower planting the soil, a householder going on a journey, a person fishing, an employer, the host at a marriage feast. In the central parable in Luke 15, between the Good Shepherd and the Prodigal Son's father, Jesus speaks of God as the homemaker who sweeps out the entire house in search of a lost coin. Job 10:10–11 speaks of God's homemaking activities as well:

> Didst thou not pour me out like milk
>   and curdle me like cheese?
> Thou didst clothe me with skin and flesh,
>   and knit me together with bones and sinews.

## GOD AS ANIMAL

Scripture portrays God not only in human images, but also in animal images. God is portrayed as an eagle. Deuteronomy 32:11 speaks of God caring for Israel

> Like an eagle that stirs up its nest,
>     that flutters over its young,
> spreading out its wings, catching them,
>     bearing them on its pinions.

Incidentally, while the King James Version uses feminine pronouns throughout the passage, subsequent translations have switched to neuter or masculine pronouns. Virginia Ramey Mollenkott suggests in *The Divine Feminine* that the eagle should be seen as one of many female images of God.

In Exodus 19:4 Yahweh instructs Moses to remind Israel "how I bore you on eagles' wings and brought you to myself." In Deuteronomy 32:11–12 and Job 39:27–30 God is again pictured as an eagle teaching its young to fly and hunt, to be self-sufficient. Eagles, who form monogamous couples both caring for the young, are said to teach the eaglets to fly by carrying them on their wings high into a draft of air, dropping them into the current, then swooping below to catch them again on their wings as they tire or flounder—a beautiful image of God nurturing us to independence.

Those who have enjoyed C. S. Lewis' Narnia series can appreciate the power of these images. In the land of Narnia God appears as Aslan, the lion (the name comes from the Turkish word for lion). At creation in *The Magician's Nephew*, the planet

> was a valley of mere earth, rock, and water; there was not a tree, not a bush, not a blade of grass to be seen. The earth was of many colours: they were fresh, hot and vivid. They made you feel excited; until you saw the Singer himself, and then you forgot everything else.
> It was a Lion. Huge, shaggy, and bright it stood facing the risen sun. Its mouth was wide open in song. (p. 101)

In *The Lion, the Witch and the Wardrobe,* after the working of "deeper magic from *before* the dawn of time," Aslan is the leader of the celebration:

> Round and round the hill-top he led them, now hopelessly out of their reach, now letting them almost catch his tail, now diving between them, now tossing them in the air with his huge and beautifully velveted paws and catching them again, and now stopping unexpectedly so that all three of them rolled over together in a happy laughing heap of fur and arms and legs. ... And the funny thing was that when all three finally lay together panting in the sun the girls no longer felt in the least tired or hungry or thirsty. (pp. 160–161)

In *The Horse and His Boy* Aslan is both the snarling lion clawing at their backs and the purring cat giving warmth and comfort among the tombs.

Lewis' inspiration undoubtedly came from references to God as the lion of the tribe of Judah (Gen. 49:9; Rev. 5:5). For the prophet Hosea, the lion-God is an image of judgment:

> For I will be like a lion to Ephraim,
>     and like a young lion to the house of Judah.
> I, even I, will rend and go away,
>     I will carry off, and none shall rescue. (5:14)
>
> ........................................
>
> So I will be to them like a lion,
>     like a leopard I will lurk beside the way.
> I will fall upon them like a bear robbed of her cubs,
>     I will tear open their breast,
> and there I will devour them like a lion,
>     as a wild beast would rend them. (13:7–8)

Incidentally, the eagle and the lion are both pictured as faces in Ezekiel's (Ezek. 1:10; 10:14) and John's visions (Rev. 4:6–7). The third face is that of an ox and the fourth that of a human being. In liturgical art these faces are often used to represent the four Gospels: Matthew the person, Mark the lion, Luke the ox, and John the eagle.

## THE INANIMATE GOD

Theologically we insist that God is a person, is personal, yet some of our most meaningful images of God are inanimate. Luther, for all of his emphasis on God's gracious love for us, wrote "A Mighty Fortress Is Our God." The hymn highlights God's protection in images of battle. In so doing, it follows Old Testament models. Psalm 91:1–2 declares,

> [The one] who dwells in the shelter of the Most High [*El Elyon*]
> who abides in the shadow of the Almighty [*Shaddai*],
> will say to the LORD [Yahweh], "My refuge and my fortress;
> my God, in whom I trust."

The psalmist goes on to combine the images of God as bird and warrior in verse 4:

> [The Lord] will cover you with [God's] pinions,
> and under [God's] wings you will find refuge;
> [The Lord's] faithfulness is a shield and buckler.

Psalm 144:2 speaks of God as "my stronghold and my deliverer" as well as "my shield."

The fortress image is most often linked to the image of God as the rock (2 Sam. 22:2; Pss. 18:2; 31:2–3; 62:2, 6; 71:3; 144:2). God as rock is a common Old Testament image. In addition to Deuteronomy 32, which we have discussed before, it appears in 1 Samuel 2:2 where Hannah sings,

> There is none holy like the LORD,
> there is none besides thee;
> there is no rock like our God.

David too sings of the rock in 2 Samuel 22:

> The LORD is my rock, and my fortress, and my deliverer,
> my God, my rock, in whom I take refuge,
> my shield and the horn of my salvation,
> my stronghold and my refuge,
> my savior; thou savest me from violence (vss. 2–3).

David returns to the image in verse 32 and again in verse 47, where he declares

> The LORD lives; and blessed be my rock,
> and exalted be my God, the rock of my salvation.

Many have taken comfort in the hymn "Beneath the Cross of Jesus," which uses the words of Isaiah 32:2 to describe the cross as

> The shadow of a mighty rock Within a weary land,
> A home within the wilderness, A rest upon the way.

Speaking of the rock which gave water to the Israelites in the wilderness, the Apostle Paul in 1 Corinthians 10:4 says, "the Rock was Christ."

Another battle image is "shield." God's opening words to Abraham in Genesis 15:1 are, "Fear not, Abram, I am your shield." Moses blesses the children of Israel in the name of the LORD,

> "the shield of your help,
> and the sword of your triumph!"(Deut. 33:29).

God is spoken of as a shield in Psalms 3:3; 28:7; 33:20; 59:11; 84:9, 11; 115:9, 10, 11; 119:114; and 144:2.

In a different set of images, God is spoken of as light, fire, and star. David begins his song of confidence with the affirmation,

> The LORD is my light and my salvation;
> whom shall I fear? (Ps. 27:1)

The prophet Micah declares that even when he sits in darkness, "the LORD will be a light to me" (Mic. 7:8). Malachi 4:2 speaks of the "sun of righteousness" rising "with healing in its wings." In describing Jesus as a "light for revelation to the Gentiles," Luke 2:32 identifies him with the one spoken of in Isaiah 42:6 as "a light to the nations." The Gospel of John repeatedly speaks of Jesus as the Light (1:4, 5, 7, 8, 9; 8:12; 9:5; 12:46; 1 John 1:5).

For the children of Israel in the wilderness that light came as a pillar of cloud by day and a pillar of fire by night (Exod. 13:21). That cloud is one of the many feminine images in

Scripture derived from the fact that *shekinah*, the cloud of God's radiance and glory, is a feminine form in Hebrew. A number of passages speak of God as the one "who rides upon the clouds" (Ps. 68:4; cf. Deut. 33:26; Ps. 33; Isa. 19:1). God appears in the fire of the burning bush (Exod. 3:2) and in the fire from heaven which consumed Elijah's sacrifice in the contest with the priests of Baal (1 Kings 18). Hebrews 12:29 says directly, "our God is a consuming fire." Lighted candles are used still today in worship to symbolize God's presence as light and fire.

Balaam's prophecy of a star out of Jacob and a scepter out of Israel (Num. 24:17) has been applied to Jesus because of the star which the seers from the east interpreted as a sign of the Messiah's coming (Matt. 2:2).

## THE GOD BEYOND WORDS

The Bible uses these and many other images to remind us that God is above, beyond, and beneath all human words. God is indeed "the living God" (1 Sam. 17:26, 36; Ps. 42:2; Hos.1:10). The mystics, those who have known God most intimately and intensely through the ages, have said the same thing. While they have struggled to put their visions into words, they have known that their experiences are beyond all words. When one contemplates the Absolute, sees the naked Godhead, experiences unconditional Love, there are no words, only awe and adoration. Our prayer should be for that vision. In the words of the hymn, we should long for that state in which all words have passed away and we are "lost in wonder, love, and praise."

## DISCUSSION:

1. A wonderful exercise to get people thinking about all of this is to go around the room and have each person give a different name or image for God. Write them all on a chalkboard or on newsprint. In doing this with seminary classes and lecture audiences, I have easily filled a whole wall of chalkboard, writing them at random.

2. Another way to approach the topic is to have each person in a study group share her or his most meaningful image of God. Refrain from assigning gender to these images. (A young woman once shared with a group that her favorite image of God was as someone who held her as she was drifting off to sleep at night. Another person in the group immediately suggested that this was an image of God as mother. It appeared to me that for a person of her age "lover" might be a much more apt label. The point is not whether either of us was correct. The point is that we each should be free to interpret our own images.)

3. Discuss the image of God as father. Why are some people so adamantly attached to it? What are its positive qualities? What might be its negative qualities for some people?

4. What new image suggested in this chapter spoke to you?

# III. Is Jesus Christ the Lord?

*I*n *All We're Meant to Be*, Letha Dawson Scanzoni and I titled a chapter "Woman's Best Friend: Jesus." Leonard Swidler wrote a rather well-known article entitled "Jesus Was a Feminist." Both have been reprinted a number of times. In *Beyond God the Father*, Mary Daly counters with a section entitled "Jesus Was a Feminist, But So What?" An article in *Christianity Today* asks the question "Is Jesus Christ a Man's Man?" and answers affirmatively. Obviously the person of Jesus Christ is at the center of the debate.

The figure Jesus raises a number of questions on a variety of levels for our discussion of language. First of all we have the male gender of the historical Jesus. How should we speak of him? How does the New Testament speak of Jesus? How has Jesus been understood historically by theologians down through the ages? What does it mean to say that in Jesus God was incarnate? Can we go further to affirm that Jesus Christ is Lord? Can we use that word? What is the theological significance of the affirmation? All are questions we must explore.

## JESUS THE MALE

The fact that Jesus was a male can be viewed in a number of ways. I have argued elsewhere that traditionally Jesus has been seen as a fulfillment of Israelite sacrificial ritual and thus as a male without spot or blemish, without sin in theological terms (although not all sacrificial animals in Jewish ritual were male). Jesus was also male in a patriarchal society because only males were allowed to teach with authority. The testimony of women was not accepted in Jewish courts, nor were women accepted as religious teachers.

In *Women, Men, and the Bible* Virginia Ramey Mollenkott has argued on a deeper level that Jesus' mission was to exemplify a new way of relating, contrary to traditional dominance-submission patterns. Jesus came as the suffering servant rather than the Davidic ruler many Jews expected (pp. 20–21). He modeled mutual submission and reciprocal respect. Only as a male could he effectively model this since women and slaves were already in submission by cultural decree.

Therefore it is both historically significant and theologically important for a feminist interpretation that Jesus was historically seen as a male. Thus the use, in moderation, of the term *man* and masculine pronouns for Jesus is appropriate. The terms should be viewed as among the historical "accidents" of Jesus' life. He was a first-century person who lived about thirty-three years in Palestine. He wore a robe and sandals; ate fish, bread, and honey; drank wine. He probably had olive complexion, brown eyes, and dark brown hair. If the evidence from the Shroud of Turin is accurate, he was about 5'11" tall and weighed approximately 178 pounds. He died by crucifixion because that was a mode of capital punishment in those days.

The problem comes in the overuse or misuse of the fact that Jesus was male. Most people would think it totally absurd to decree that only persons 5'11" tall could be leaders in a Christian community, yet many agree with Pope Paul VI that only males can be ordained because of their "natural resemblance" to Jesus. To state it more precisely, the problem arises when people use Jesus' maleness to identify men with him in a way which excludes women.

Take, for instance, the article "Was Jesus Christ a Man's Man?" The author Vivian Clark declares:

> It is helpful to look at the male aspect of Jesus Christ in his humanity, for he portrayed a theology of maleness. He was a picture of masculinity, a role model for boys to follow as they grow up learning to be men. His relationship to his Father, his understanding of himself, and his involvement with others paint for us a picture worth our study.

Reread the paragraph substituting *female, her, she, femininity, girls, women,* and *Mother.* If Jesus does not offer a theology applicable to femaleness and a model for girls to follow as they grow up as well, then females might just as well start shopping for a different religion because they are excluded from this one. Many women, indeed, have come to this conclusion at precisely this point.

But was this the intention of the historical Jesus or of the founders of the Christian faith? Even though all our records were written within a patriarchal culture and handed down in a religious institution with clearly patriarchalizing biases and intentions, we still have no record of Jesus asserting his maleness or putting down women as female. Dorothy Sayers said it so well in her essay "The Human-Not-Quite-Human?":

> Perhaps it is no wonder that the women were first at the Cradle and last at the Cross. They had never known a man like this Man—there never has been such another. A prophet and teacher who never nagged at them, never flattered or coaxed or patronised; who never made arch jokes about them, never treated them either as "The women, God help us!" or "The ladies, God bless them!"; who rebuked without querulousness and praised without condescension; who took their questions and arguments seriously; who never mapped out their sphere for them, never urged them to be feminine or jeered at them for being female; who had no axe to grind and no uneasy male dignity to defend; who took them as he found them and was completely unself-conscious. There is no act, no sermon, no parable in the whole Gospel that borrows its pungency from female perversity; nobody could possibly guess from the words and

deeds of Jesus that there was anything "funny" about woman's nature. (p. 47)

As she notes, however, "God, of course, may have His own opinion, but the Church is reluctant to endorse it!" (p. 46).

## JESUS THE PERSON

The early church was fairly clear that Jesus' significance in the proclamation of the gospel was as *anthropos*, a person, a human being, and not as *aner*, a man, a male. In Jesus, God became human, flesh, not male. For example, in the Gospels Jesus' opponents labeled him "a man [*anthropos*] gluttonous, and a winebibber, a friend of publicans and sinners" (Mat. 11:19; Luke 7:34 KJV). In the story of the healing of the man born blind in John 9, again Jesus' opponents referred to him repeatedly as *anthropos*: "This man [*anthropos*] is not from God, for he does not keep the sabbath. . . How can a man [*anthropos*] who is a sinner do such signs? . . . we know that this man [*anthropos*] is a sinner" (9:16, 24; cf. John 11:47). They accuse him of blasphemy "because you, being a man [*anthropos*], make yourself God" (John 10:33). The officers acknowledge, however, that "No man [*anthropos*] ever spoke like this man [*anthropos*]!" (John 7:46).

Throughout the Passion narratives, Jesus is referred to as *anthropos*. Pilate declares, "You brought me this man [*anthropos*] as one who was perverting the people; and after examining him before you, behold, I did not find this man [*anthropos*] guilty of any of your charges against him" (Luke 23:14; cf. Luke 23:4, 6; John 18:29). John records Pilate as declaring, "Here is the man [*anthropos*]" (19:5). The centurion, after Jesus' death, exclaims; "Truly this man [*anthropos*] was a Son of God!" (Mark 15:39: cf. Luke 23:47). Each of these references could be translated more accurately as "person."

The writers of the Epistles also use *anthropos* for the most part when referring to the incarnation. The writer of 1 Corinthians draws an interesting parallel in 15:21 and 47: "For as by a man [*anthropou*] came death, by a man [*anthropou*] has come also the resurrection of the dead. . . . The first man [*anthropos*] was from the earth, [earthy], the second man [*anthropos*] is from heaven" (the RSV translates earthy as "man of dust"). The writer of Philippians, in the great exposition of the incarnation, says that we are to emulate Christ who "emptied himself, taking the form of a servant, being born in the likeness of men [*anthropon*]. And being found in human [*anthropos*] form he humbled himself and became obedient unto death, even death on a cross" (Phil, 2:7–8). Even the later writer of 1 Timothy 2:5 puts it most bluntly: "For there is one God, and there is one mediator between God and men [*anthropon*], the man [*anthropos*] Christ Jesus."

Only a few instances appear to refer to Jesus' maleness: John 1:30; Acts 2:22; 17:31; Ephesians 4:13. In John 1:30 John the Baptist announces that "After me comes a man [*aner*] who ranks before me." In Acts 2:22 Peter in his sermon at Pentecost, which is rather curiously addressed to male Jews, *andres Israelitai* (cf. 2:14, 22, 29, 37; cf. also 3:12, 17; 7:2, 26; 13:16, 26, 38; 15:7, 13; 17:22; 19:35; 21:28; 22:1; 23:1, 6; 28:17), refers to "Jesus of Nazareth, a man [*andra*] attested to you by God with mighty works and wonders and signs." Later in Acts Paul, preaching likewise to male Athenians (17:22), refers to Jesus as "a man [*andri*] whom [God] has appointed, and of this [God] has given assurance to all [RSV adds "men" here] by raising him from the dead" (vs. 31). Ephesians 4:13 is a very interesting case because the writer has been arguing precisely that in Christ human divisions have been overcome and the Christian community is one in Christ, yet at the culmination of the passage the author urges Christians to grow "until we all attain to the unity of the faith and of the knowledge of the Son of God, to mature manhood [*andra teleion*], to the measure of the stature of the fullness of Christ." The point here appears to be an emphasis not on Jesus' maleness, but on maturity, adulthood. In the patriarchal society of the first century, only freeborn males had all the rights and privileges of mature adulthood. This idea is underscored by the next verse, which goes on to say "that we may no longer be children, tossed to and fro."

The overwhelming use of *anthropos*, however, does suggest that the early Christian community, despite strong patriarchalizing pressures, maintained the distinction, clearly teaching that in the historical Jesus, God became *human*. This teaching is also the intention of the debates which resulted in the writing of the creeds. In the Nicene Creed we are still forced in English to declare that in Jesus Christ God "was made man" although again the Greek originally had *anthropos* and the Latin *homo* (rather than the more specifically male *vir*). I personally always say "human" because I feel that if Jesus did not become human, then I as a woman have no hope of salvation. The International Consultation on English Texts (ICET), which revised the creeds for common use, did at least pare down the previous phrase which declared explicitly that the incarnation was "for us *men* [italics added] and for our salvation." That too originally read *"di hemas tous anthropous"* or *"qui propter nos homines."* It now reads "for us and for our salvation."

## JESUS AS SON

References to Jesus as Son of God and Son of Man are also troublesome. Capitalizing them at least alerts us to the fact that they are titles used in Scripture and not intended as literal statements of biological relationship. They are titles with a rich history in apocalyptic literature and come from there into the Gospels, which means we cannot just dispense with them. On the other hand, capitalizing them makes them even more obvious and offensive in their maleness. As we have seen in the discussion of God as Father, the titles of Father and Son are intended to point to the character of the unique relationship between God and Jesus, not to the maleness of that relationship in the human analogy. Ironically the images of Son of God and "only begotten son" draw their power from patriarchal, patrilinear culture in which primogeniture, the right of inheritance of the firstborn son, influences all social relationships. Primogeniture is, of course, no longer the rule in our society.

To argue for the importance of the terms *father* and *son* on the basis that Jesus is the male offspring of God the Father and the Virgin Mary is, as I have said before, to reduce profound theological mysteries to the level of pagan, primitive mythology. The point of the title *Son of God* is to affirm that Jesus was, in the words of the Nicene Creed,

> eternally begotten of the Father,
> God from God, Light from Light,
> true God from true God,
> begotten, not made,
> of one Being with the Father.

The title is intended to point to Jesus' identity with God rather than to his maleness.

In the sense that Jesus was truly human, Mary was his single and sole parent, mother and father. The Third Council of Toledo (589) affirmed that in the sense of truly divine, God was both father and mother, that Jesus was born *de utero patris*, from the father's womb. As a conservative scientist, Edward L. Kessel, has argued in the evangelical *Journal of the American Scientific Affiliation*, if one believes that Jesus was literally born as the product of a virgin birth, then he was chromosomally female, though phenotypically male. On the psychological level, it has long been recognized that while our culture has sex-role stereotypes which decree rather divergent behavior for men and women, Jesus modeled a humanity which encompassed both. The New Testament affirms a goal of Christ-likeness for all Christians, without any gender distinctions.

The *Inclusive Language Lectionary* translates Son of God as "Child of God." While this de-emphasizes the male reference, it does raise several questions. For one thing, the New Testament does have a word for son, *huios,* and others for child, *paidion* and *teknon.* Thus in the lectionary we have a problem of literal accuracy, though translators have not always been particularly scrupulous in their treatment of these words (see Chapter VI concerning translation). Basically the words seem to be used somewhat interchangeably.

The other problem with Child of God is one of connotation: all human beings are the children of God; certainly all Christians think of themselves as the children of God. Some have also objected to the use of "Child of God" on grounds that it implies perpetual immaturity. While this is a valid point, one does refer even to adults as "the children of so-and-so" when discussing relationship. In fact most of the New Testament references to children are of this type, and adults are spoken of as children of a certain leader. And the Bible clearly encourages growth to adult maturity even in relationship to God.

Likewise, the title Son of Man is intended to point to Jesus' identity with humanity rather than to his maleness. Since the term translated Man is always *anthropos*, the phrase could at least be translated Son of Humanity or Child of Humanity. Heir of God and Heir of Humanity are also possibilities since the term *son* is not intended to convey immaturity but the ability to receive the fullness of God's gift (cf. Gal. 3:15–4:31). The *Inclusive Language Lectionary* chooses to translate this title as the "Human One," pointing to Jesus as the archetypal person, and thus conveys the intended meaning of the title.

## THE CHRIST

Christians affirm that Jesus, very God, is the Christ, the Messiah, the Anointed One. This is an important title and can be used somewhat interchangeably with Jesus by the careful writer and speaker, depending on whether one is talking about the historical or the theological figure.

The title can be particularly attractive to feminists who ask, who anointed Jesus? Most theologians would quickly answer, God. Jesus was God's Chosen One, God's Appointed One. Yet biblical scholars might more cautiously note that on the human level, just as the prophet Nathan anointed Saul and David as kings of Israel, it was a woman who physically anointed Jesus. John 12:1–8 says that he was anointed by Mary of Bethany six days before Passover, during a supper at the home of Mary, Martha, and Lazarus (cf. Mark 14:3–9; Matt. 26:6–13). In Luke 7:37 it was "a woman of the city, who was a sinner" who did the anointing. In either case, it was certainly a female who carried out the physical act of signifying God's action. Using the same words as he did in instituting holy communion, Jesus declared that "wherever this gospel is preached in the whole world, what she has done will be told in memory of her" (Matt. 26:13).

## *JESUS OUR ALL*

Scripture offers a wealth of other titles for Jesus, which can enrich our understanding and proclamation, particularly from the "I am" passages in John's Gospel. Using metaphorical language, Jesus spoke of himself as "living water" (John 4:10); "the bread of life" (6:35,48); "the bread which came down from heaven" (6:41); "food indeed and . . . drink indeed" (6:55); "the light of the world" (8:12; 9:5); the "I AM" (8:58); "the door of the sheep" (10:7); "the good shepherd" (10:11,14); "the resurrection and the life" (11:25); "the way, and the truth, and the life" (14:6); "the true vine" (15:1,5). Jesus was also addressed as master and teacher. He was called friend and the bridegroom.

One of the most important names is the Word, the *Logos*, used in John 1:1. This is a word of masculine grammatical gender and corresponds to the Hebrew concept of Wisdom, *Hokmah*, which is of feminine grammatical gender in Hebrew and personified as female in the book of Proverbs:

> Wisdom cries aloud in the street;
>   in the markets she raises her voice. (1:20)
>
> Get wisdom; get insight.
> Do not forsake her, and she will keep you;
>   love her, and she will guard you. (4:5–6)
>
> Wisdom has built her house,
>   she has set up her seven pillars. (9:1)

Wisdom is *Sophia* in Greek, another term of feminine grammatical gender.

In hymnody images such as the lily of the valley, the bright and morning star, and the fairest of ten thousand are usually applied to Jesus, though they are taken from Old Testament references. Similarly many apply Isaiah's texts concerning the Suffering Servant to Jesus.

We can also refer to Jesus in terms suggested by his life: the Galilean, the Nazarene, the Carpenter, the Crucified One, the Resurrected One, our Redeemer, our Redemption. The motto of the Christian and Missionary Alliance Church, in which I grew up, is Jesus Christ: Savior, Sanctifier, Healer, and Coming King. Aimee Semple McPherson defined her Foursquare Gospel in essentially the same terms. Since *king* is also a masculine reference, we could just as easily say sovereign, which would fit the alliteration in those mottoes better anyway. Of course, many of the descriptions of God have also been applied to Jesus as well.

## IS JESUS LORD?

Throughout the New Testament Jesus is also referred to as Lord. The key declaration for early Christians was, "Jesus Christ is Lord!" The martyrs, male and female, died for that affirmation. It was central to their faith; thus we must take it with utmost seriousness.

Many feminists today, concerned for the use of inclusive language, object to the use of the term *Lord* as a male term corresponding to the term *Lady* and used of the upper classes particularly in England. This is a valid point and one certainly most obvious to those who reside in the present or former British Empire. This is another case in which English uses two distinct words connoting gender, whereas in Greek the word *kyrios*, meaning the supreme authority, could, with a feminine ending, be used of a woman as well—see 2 John 1, 5. The word could also mean an owner of possessions, the head of a household, or the master of slaves. In the vocative, it meant the equivalent of *sir* or *ma'am*. It is the term the Philippian jailer used to address Paul and Silas in Acts 16:30; the King James Version translates it "Sirs" and the Revised Standard Version "Men, what must I do to be saved?" Thus when 1 Peter 3:6 suggests that Sarah called Abraham "lord," she was not confusing him with God.

After the Evangelical Women's Caucus had published its statement of faith, it received a number of questions from sincere biblical feminists about the statement concerning "Jesus Christ as Lord and Savior." The responses objected to the term Lord, not the concept of Christ's sovereignty. Discussing the issue at length, several of us noted that we personally do not find the term offensive since it is not one commonly used in American society, thus making it one which a person can reserve exclusively for God. Yet we sympathized with the intent behind the questions.

I came away from the discussion still using the term Lord personally and not wanting to abandon it totally in public worship. During the 1983 Bicentennial Consultation on Wesleyan Theology and the Next Century at Emory University, the feminist theology group discussed the issue. Rosemary Radford Ruether reminded us that the initial theological intent of the affirmation that Jesus Christ is Lord was to say the Jesus is God and no one else is. The martyrs died because they considered Jesus to be God, but they did not believe any emperor who proclaimed himself divine, to be God. Thus to say that Jesus Christ is Lord is precisely to affirm that no man, no human being, is. Therefore, for today's woman the affirmation that Jesus Christ is Lord can be precisely the same kind of attack on patriarchal structures as it was for the early Christians.

The *Inclusive Language Lectionary* initially used "Sovereign" or the "Sovereign One" instead of Lord, and this certainly is an accurate, adequate translation. In fact, to say that Jesus is Sovereign has a nuance that we intend but sometimes lose in the familiar "Jesus is Lord." To say Jesus is Sovereign carries both the idea of a verb—that Jesus is constantly ruling—and the idea of a predicate noun—that Jesus is indeed ruler over all. As they have continued their work, however, the Inclusive Language Lectionary Committee decided to include "Lord" in brackets as an alternate reading in all places where it appears in the Revised Standard Version.

Some have argued that theologically we must be careful to guard the acknowledgment of God's sovereignty, to preserve an understanding of God's transcendence in this day when we value intimacy so highly and sometimes almost trivialize God in our emphasis on immanence. Certainly as I have argued repeatedly in this book, we need to remember all aspects of our knowledge of God's nature and to expand that knowledge. On the other hand, God does not need our defense. God simply is! We who feel our weakness and vulnerability sometimes need to bolster our strength and confidence, but God who rules the universe came to this earth as a helpless babe in a manger. We who feel powerless become defensive, but God who is omnipotent became in Jesus Christ powerless and defenseless to the point of death on the cross. It is we as human beings who have "control issues." God, who truly is in control, who is Cosmic Process, does not worry about being in control. Jesus did not ask his disciples to defend him but to follow him. God is not threatened by our freedom; God is not limited by our limitations.

Jesus was a historical person of male gender. Jesus Christ, Christians affirm, is also the author and finisher of our faith, God in human form, deity made flesh. As Gregory the Great argued, what is not assumed cannot be redeemed. If Jesus was not, as Christian and Missionary Alliance founder A.B. Simpson argued in the nineteenth century, just as much a woman as a man, then Jesus is not woman's redeemer. Scripture, however, emphasizes Christ's humanity, not his maleness or masculinity. It also offers us a variety of ways of speaking of the divine in human form. To affirm that uniqueness, to affirm indeed that Jesus is Sovereign is to strike at the heart of patriarchal dominance.

### DISCUSSION:

1. How have you usually thought of or pictured Jesus in your own relationship with him?

2. Why do you think that Jesus as God Incarnate was a male?

3. What is the theological meaning of the Incarnation? What does it mean to say that in Jesus God became as one of us?

4. What is your favorite image of Jesus from his teachings?

5. Discuss the phrases *Son of God* and *Son of Man*. What do you think they are supposed to mean? What do you think of the *Inclusive Language Lectionary*'s choice of substitutes? Can you think of other possible translations?

# IV. Spirit and Triune

$G$od, of course, is Spirit, as Jesus told the woman at the well in Samaria (John 4:24). We affirm that, and yet we often forget the work of the Holy Spirit.

For those concerned about inclusive language, the Spirit presents several problems—and several new solutions. In Hebrew and Aramaic, Jesus' native tongue, the word for Spirit, *ruach,* which also means breath or wind, is feminine in gender. The Greek word, *pneuma,* is neuter. Thus to speak of the Holy Spirit as he is incorrect. We can more accurately speak of the Spirit as she or it (and so pronouns referring to the Spirit should be translated in Scripture).

The choice of pronouns raises an issue which troubles many about this whole matter. They note that we believe that God is a *person,* and thus we must use personal pronouns to speak of God, *he* or *she* but never *it.* Actually this is simply a trap in the English language. Some languages offer personal pronouns of indefinite gender. Some languages do not have personal pronouns.

God is Spirit; the third person of the Trinity is the Holy Spirit. In Scripture, a number of images are used for the Spirit, many of them feminine. Some have argued that we could speak of the other two members of the Trinity as male and the Spirit as female. While such a solution might be tempting, it is ultimately unbiblical because it again assigns gender to God, which Hebrew religion opposed vehemently. As Virginia Ramey Mollenkott has consistently argued in both *Women, Men, and the Bible* and *The Divine Feminine*, all persons of the Trinity are described in Scripture using both masculine and feminine images.

In the beginning it was the Spirit of God, a feminine noun, which was "moving"—hovering, brooding, or literally fluttering—over the face of the waters (Gen. 1:2). In the Old Testament the Spirit is often identified with the pillar of cloud by day and the pillar of fire by night which led the children of Israel in their wilderness wanderings (Exod. 13:21–22). This is identified with the *Shekinah*, another feminine gender word for God's presence which dwelt in the Tabernacle, especially around the Ark of the Covenant. The Spirit appears as divine energy and power. The Spirit is the One who empowers us with intelligence and skill (Exod. 31:3), physical strength (Judg. 14:6), and leadership abilities (Judg. 3:10). The Spirit is also the One who speaks through the prophets (Isa. 63:10–11).

In the New Testament the Spirit in the form of a dove descended upon Jesus at his baptism (Matt. 3:16). At Pentecost the Spirit fell upon the men and women assembled in the Upper Room in the form of a mighty rushing wind and tongues of fire (Acts 2:2–4).

Jesus, in promising to send the Holy Spirit, described it as the Comforter, the Counselor, the Spirit of Truth, the Advocate (John 14:16, 26; 16:7–14). The Greek word is *Paraclete*.

Paul in Galatians 5:23–24 lists the fruits of the Spirit's activity in a person's life as "love, joy, peace, patience, kindness, goodness, faithfulness, gentleness, self-control." The Spirit is responsible for a person's spiritual growth to maturity, and the Spirit gives gifts to individual Christians for the upbuilding of the church (1 Cor. 12:11).

In art the Spirit is most often represented by the descending dove. Other representations include a sevenfold flame or tongues of fire, the seven-branched candlestick or *menorah*, and seven lamps representing the seven gifts of the Spirit—wisdom, understanding, counsel, strength, knowledge, true godliness, and holy fear or awe.

## THREE IN ONE

While the concept of the Trinity is not delineated in Scripture, the church in its affirmation that Jesus was truly divine worked out a belief in a Triune God, three equal persons in unity. In art it is symbolized by the equilateral triangle or the circle, separately or intertwined, the trefoil or the triquetra, and sometimes three fish entwined. The three persons are equal; they are not to be identified with each other or separated from each other; they are not to be subordinated one to another. They do not represent a hierarchy.

Using scriptural insights and visions which were given her by God, Dame Julian of Norwich meditated at length on the triune God. In both the short and long versions of her *Showings* (or *Revelations of Divine Love*, as they have been titled), she repeatedly speaks of the Trinity: "the Creator and the lover and the protector" of all that is (p. 131); "almighty, all wise and all good" (p. 132); "sovereign power, sovereign wisdom, sovereign goodness" (p. 164); "the property of the fatherhood, and the property of the motherhood, and the property of the lordship in one God" (p. 293); "the high might of the Trinity is our Father, and the deep wisdom of the Trinity is our Mother, and the great love of the Trinity is our Lord" (p. 294); "our Father wills, our Mother works, our good Lord the Holy Spirit confirms" (p. 296).

The essence of the Trinity is community, a fellowship of mutuality and love. It serves as a model for us. The primary relationship between human beings was not intended to be the marital couple or the nuclear family; thus our God is not a dyad of husband and wife or a triad of mother, father, and child. The model is friendship. While One, God is not solitary. The Trinity is a relationship of three coinherent persons.

## SPEAKING AND WRITING ABOUT GOD

Many people are comfortable with male language about God, and changing seems scripturally incompatible, historically inaccurate, practically difficult, and psychologically abhorrent. In reality it is none of the above. If it does not seem worthwhile, you might practice saying, "In the name of God the Mother, God the Daughter, and God the Holy Spirit." I am not suggesting that the church adopt this formula at all, but if it startles and offends you, perhaps you get a bit of the feeling many women have about traditional language.

One frequently hears the objection, "Changing language about people is one thing and I don't object to that, but changing language about God is something altogether different." True. Theological precision is a very serious matter, particularly for those who are committed to a religion with historical sources of revelation. Certain Christian theological formulations are indelibly masculine, most notably the trinitarian formula of "Father, Son, and Holy Ghost" used in baptism and blessings. One must respect that and seek to understand it within its historical, philosophical, and cultural context. One must equally respect particularly the Old Testament commands against identifying God with any specific image and against portraying the God of Israel in ways similar to the anthropomorphic gods of the surrounding peoples. One must also take seriously the multiplicity of the biblical revelation concerning God. Elevating one image or group of images to the exclusion of the others is idolatry.

Yahweh, the Most High God, is not some white Anglo-Saxon Protestant male American tribal deity. Our language should reflect the richness of our biblical heritage and theological beliefs.

So, how does one go about it? Chapter VII on worship has a number of suggestions, but here are a few principles. Be specific and use the biblical resources we have. If the topic is creation, speak of the Creator. If it is salvation, speak of the Savior, Redeemer, Sanctifier. If the objective is to bring comfort to the sick or grieving, speak of the Comforter, the Mother, the

Shepherd, the Great Physician, the One who mourns with us.

Avoid masculine pronouns or balance them with feminine pronouns. One simple solution used in the *Inclusive Language Lectionary* is to repeat "God." Many here object that this becomes redundant. How strange that we never felt that way about using *he* three or four times in the same sentence. One can follow the biblical example of alternating various names of God. Sentences can usually be recast to take care of this problem. For example, "God's goodness is seen in his dealings with his people" can easily become "The Lord's goodness is evident in the Almighty's dealings with God's people." Often one can also simply eliminate possessive pronouns. For example, the sentence "God is revealed in his creation" can just as clearly read "God is revealed in creation"—we know it is God's.

Above all do not capitalize pronouns referring to God. Most publishers have already eliminated this practice because it is a relic of earlier styles of punctuation which capitalized many more words than we do today, perhaps based on the German practice of capitalizing all nouns. While one may use male pronouns for Jesus and occasionally for God, in general when one cannot creatively find a way around it, one need not advertise the fact with capitalization. For those sensitive to language issues, capitalizing the pronouns totally fogs the windows of the spirit, even when reading an otherwise excellent book. It reinforces a woman's feeling of being an intruder into what is apparently a male-only world.

One rather creative solution is to alternate male and female pronouns for God. Now perhaps this sounds a bit bizarre, but Dody Donnelly has done it in *Radical Love*. The alternation is not done mechanically by occurrence or sentence or paragraph, but by topic or thought. Thus throughout the discussion of one idea she uses male pronouns for the deity; then throughout the next point she uses female pronouns. The result is both readable and refreshing.

A particular problem is the reflexive *himself*. One suggestion is to adopt the word *Godself*. This works in a sentence such as "God made us for Godself." It does not work as well in a sentence like "God himself is at work in our lives." One suggestion here is to adopt the language of Scripture and creed to say "God, very God, is at work in our lives." Or one can achieve the same emphasis by doubling the names of God as in "God Almighty is at work in our lives."

If making changes in the way we speak of God seems too difficult and not worth the bother, we need to remember that we are speaking of the One we say we worship and we are influencing our own souls and the souls of others. If God is the One to whom our lives are ultimately committed, then we should be willing to endure a bit of bother! Indeed we should enjoy the exercise of thinking more deeply and creatively about our God, of expressing more eloquently and persuasively what we feel and believe about the One we love and worship.

## DISCUSSION:

1. How do you picture and experience the Holy Spirit? Speaking of the "Holy Ghost" has given many of us a very fuzzy picture of the third person of the Trinity. How would you make it more precise, using Scripture, experience, tradition?

2. Draw a diagram of your understanding of the Trinity.

3. Use the Apostles' and Nicene creeds to explore how the church has defined the persons and relationships within the Trinity.

4. Using more inclusive language, rewrite the following paragraph from Richard J. Foster's *Celebration of Discipline:*

> We worship the Lord not only because of who He is but also because of what He has done. Above all, the God of the Bible is the God who acts. His goodness, faithfulness, justice, mercy all can be seen in His dealings with His people. His gracious actions are not only etched into ancient history, but are engraved into our personal histories. As the apostle Paul said, the only reasonable response is worship (Rom. 12:1). We praise God for who He is, and thank Him for what He has done. (p. 140)

5. Have you seen other creative ways of dealing with pronouns? Can you suggest any?

# V. Is Man Human?

*H*uman language is a product of culture and is continually evolving. We can see that very easily by comparing the King James Version of the Bible with more recent translations and paraphrases. For example, compare the first two verses of Psalm 44 in the King James and Today's English Versions:

> We have heard with our ears, O God, our fathers have told us, what work thou didst in their days, in the times of old.
>
> How thou didst drive out the heathen with thy hand, and plantedst them; how thou didst afflict the people, and cast them out.

> With our own ears we have heard it, O God—
>     our ancestors have told us about it,
> about the great things you did in their time,
>     in the days of long ago:
> how you yourself drove out the heathen
>     and established your people in their land;
> how you punished the other nations
>     and caused your own to prosper.

We no longer use "thou" or "didst" or "plantedst." Psalm 42:2 no longer says "My soul thirsteth for God," but simply "I thirst for you, the living God." "Hath" is now "has"; "art" is "are."

The Episcopal Church revised the Book of Common Prayer in the nineteen-seventies in part because while the language inherited from Queen Elizabeth I's day was beautiful, it no longer communicated accurately. For example, when the minister intoned after the confession, "Hear what comfortable words our Lord Jesus Christ has to say," people were not supposed to get cozy but to be comforted or encouraged by the fact that their sins were forgiven.

We all recognize that while our grandparents described something as the cat's meow and we thought it was cool, our children are more likely to describe it as totally awesome. We also are aware that within our own lifetime such enterprises as the space program, medicine, nuclear energy, computer technology, and bioengineering have added whole crops of new words to our vocabularies. Thus language is not static but ever changing and expanding.

Similarly, grammar also shifts and changes. English teachers are well aware of different systems for teaching grammar. Textbooks from different publishers often label grammatical concepts differently—predicate nominative and subject complement, for example, are two terms for the same concept. Many of the rules of good writing which we were taught in school were the personal preferences of nineteenth-century grammarians who set out to bring order to American grammar, which differed considerably from region to region and from British usage.

One rule in particular which is apropos our current topic was the grammarians' insistence that a singular indefinite or collective noun should be followed by a singular masculine pronoun. This rule was established in England in 1850 by an Act of Parliament which declared that *he* is generic and legally includes *she*. Parliament merely followed a rule invented in 1746 by John Kirby, who decreed that the male gender is "more comprehensive" than the female. Thus one should say, "Everyone should bring *his* own lunch." Prior to that decision, it was perfectly acceptable to say, "Everyone should bring their own lunch." As a result, for example, Dr. Benjamin Spock's *Baby and Child Care* for years referred to the child as "he" as though girl babies did not exist. This one seemingly insignificant grammatical rule, which we all grew up believing was engraved in stone somewhere, has rendered women invisible in textbooks, medical books, instruction manuals, newspapers—everywhere in print. Many contemporary writers are now returning to the former usage of "their." After all, it was good enough for Shakespeare!

While many men assume that we all understand that the "he" is generic in such sentences as "A historian must be careful about how he uses his sources," as a female historian I can say that such references hammer home in a young scholar grave doubts as to whether or not she can ever be a *real* historian. Certainly enough battles have been waged over women's ordination in church conventions to illustrate the point that when one refers to ministerial candidates as he and him, most people do not understand these pronouns to include women. If you still consider *he* as generic, try to draft a memo urging each secretary to be at his desk promptly at 9 A.M. each morning.

When the woman's movement began to regroup in the nineteen-sixties, inclusive language became an early issue. One of the first areas to be examined was school textbooks. A cursory reading readily revealed that girls were underrepresented and often negatively represented in subject and illustration as well as language. Parents concerned about the negative pictures of women and girls being conveyed by their children's textbooks urged publishers to include more stories with girls as heroes, more illustrations of girls and women in a positive light, more historical references to the achievements of women. At the same time many readers were also concerned with the treatment of people of color. Many texts contained few if any references to or pictures of nonwhite children or adults. Parents also urged writers to word material in such a way that both boys and girls could identify with it, rather than wording it to imply that white men were the only actors and intended audience.

One of the first publishers to respond was McGraw-Hill, which put out a set of guidelines for writers that became an industry standard. Soon other publishers followed suit. Now even the prestigious Modern Language Association advocates use of inclusive language. The government revised job titles from designations such as fireman and salesman to fire fighter and sales representative because male designations encouraged businesses to think of such jobs as for men only and discouraged women from applying.

Most of us have grown used to such changes in the past twenty years. Few of us would like to return to having newspaper want ads again labeled Men and Women as they used to be, any more than we would tolerate going back to the days when drinking fountains were labeled white and colored. We have become accustomed to believing that, regardless of color or gender, children should take whatever classes interest them, that they should aspire to whatever careers they desire, and that any person who has the training and skills for a job should apply for it.

We have accepted, even welcomed these changes in society, rightly realizing that they have enriched our lives and will enrich our children's lives. Yet many Christians resist such changes in the church and home. Ironically they favor social justice but not religious and domestic equity. Indeed this gives many people outside the church the false impression that God is the author of oppression rather than freedom.

## WHO IS A MAN?

In the far distant past there may have been a time when the word *man* meant both male and female, but it has been clear for some time now that I as a female cannot properly designate myself as a "man." It does not take a diagram on the door to tell me that a room labeled Men is not meant for me. The term is no longer generic in ordinary usage. For religious leaders to suggest that one should continue to read it and hear it as generic in religious contexts is similar to arguing that services should continue to be conducted in Greek or Latin or German even when not a soul in the congregation understands the language.

When we read the theological and devotional writings of the past, we assume that *man* and *men* were used generically to mean all persons. When I taught courses in the theology of John Wesley, I required students to write successive short papers on half a dozen of his theological concepts. Somewhat jokingly I told them that I would allow them to use sexist language in the first paper on sin in such phrases as "all men are sinners" but that by the time we got to the concepts of salvation and sanctification, I expected them to be including women in their language. Wesley himself gives us a glaring example of just how slippery the supposedly generic use of *man* can become. In a letter to a Dr. Conyers Middleton contrasting the evidence given by Christian tradition with the internal witness of the Spirit, Wesley declares:

> Traditional evidence is of an extremely complicated nature, necessarily including so many and so various considerations, that only men of a strong and clear understanding can be sensible of its full force. On the contrary, how plain and simple is this [internal evidence]! and how level to the lowest capacity! Is not this the sum—"One thing I know; I was blind, but now I see"? An argument so plain, that a peasant, a woman, a child may feel all its force. (*Letters*, ed. Telford, 2:384)

Even though in general Wesley, deeply influenced by the wisdom of his mother Susanna, was very supportive of women and encouraged their ministry, his words betray the residual prejudices of his culture. His ministry also deeply affected the mine workers, the urban poor, the lower classes throughout England, and yet his classism and educational elitism also show here. This quotation illustrates how one may assume that common nouns such as peasants, immigrants, pioneers, Christians, and so on, include men and women, only to be brought up short by a specific reference to women or wives. It also shows how easily we betray our lack of inclusivity even when we are trying to be inclusive.

Indeed, Hebrew has three words translated "man": *'adam*, which means person; *'enosh*, which means mortal; and *'ish*, which means male (*'ishshah* means female). Greek makes a distinction between *anthropos*, human being, and *aner* (stem form *andr-*), man or husband (*gyne* means woman or wife), though translators have not maintained this distinction either. The Latin *homo sapiens* certainly refers to all human beings because again *homo* means man and woman with *mas* and *vir* reserved for the male while *femina* and *mulier* refer to woman (though the first syllable from the words *homonym*, *homogeneous*, and *homosexual* come from the Greek root meaning same). However, the English word *man* comes from the Teutonic branch of Indo-European and is related to *mensch* in German, *menneske* in Danish and Norwegian, and *manniska* in Swedish. These still retain their inclusive meaning of person, male or female, adult or child. Sometimes spelled *mann* or *monn*, when *man* first appeared in English it was clearly inclusive. Aelfric, in about 1000, wrote: "His mother was a Christian, named Elen, a very full-of-faith man, and extremely pious." A sermon in 1597 declared that "The Lord had put but one pair of men in Paradise" (spelling modernized).

At that time English also had separate words to designate the two genders: *weapman* and *carlman* for an adult male person and *wifman* for an adult female person. Eventually *wifman* became *woman* and *wif* became *wife*, but *wer* and *weapmen*, *carl* and *carlman* disappeared altogether. And *man* became ambiguous (for a fuller discussion see Casey Miller and Kate Swift, *Words and Women*, pp. 24–25).

The use of the slippery generic was brought home to me initially by a sermon one day in chapel at Trinity College, Deerfield, Illinois, where I was teaching English. The minister's second point was "God needs gifted men." Preaching from Ephesians 4, he was stressing that those who have been given gifts—"that some should be apostles, some prophets, some evangelists, some pastors and teachers, for the equipment of the saints, for the work of ministry, for building up the body of Christ" (Eph. 4:11–12)—should use those gifts to serve God. Afterward I asked if he had intended his point about God needing gifted "men" to be taken generically. He assured me he did. I went on to suggest that since more than half the students were women that it would have been nice if at least once in a while he had said, "God needs gifted men and women" or "gifted people." I then noted that I was glad that he supported women in the ordained ministry. Suddenly he became flustered. He blurted out that of course he did not believe in the ordination of women! It instantly became clear that despite his attempts at camouflage, he did mean that "God needs gifted men" and not women.

We say that *men* in Scripture, for example, includes women, yet in discussions about the biblical role of women, only those passages which specifically say "woman" or "women" are examined. Similarly the works of theologians are combed for those instances in which they speak specifically about women, and all of their other theological insights are ignored as though they do not apply to women. Using the words *man* or *men* only provides an illusion of inclusion. In reality we can only be sure that women are included when they are specifically addressed.

Yet to include women as well as men is simply a matter of justice. Together we form the human race—it is not *man*kind but humanity, humankind (*human* comes from the Latin *humus*, or ground, and thus *humanus, humanity*). We are not all men but persons, people, men and women. We are not just the "brethren," but brothers and sisters in Christ. How can we begin to reflect the whole body of Christ in our language about each other?

## LOVE ONE ANOTHER

A frequent message of the New Testament is that Christians are to be "forbearing one another in love" (Eph. 4:2), to "outdo one another in showing honor" (Rom. 12:10), to "be subject to one another out of reverence for Christ" (Eph. 5:21).

Yet we often demean one another by our words. Most of us are well aware of how Black people have been stigmatized by such words as *nigger, colored, boy,* or *mammy.* In very few churches today would a minister of the gospel tell a racist story. Yet some still find it acceptable to tell jokes demeaning to women. Some still refer to women as girls no matter what their age, even though *girl* is a term that usually refers only to female children. Originally it meant all children (Miller and Swift, p. 87).

Some men (and some women) also have difficulty understanding the objection to calling women "ladies." The word can certainly be a term of respect, in statements such as "she was a real lady," but it generally carries connotations of the upper class, the leisured class. It suggests that women are ornaments or decorations rather than real people. It also suggests that the only proper behavior for women is whatever the speaker deems "ladylike." Think about the differences implied in the injunctions "Act like a lady!" and "Be a man!" The concept of being a lady has been used to put women on pedestals in an effort to keep them out of the marketplace.

In a related matter, many people bridle at saying or writing anything besides *chairman.* Some women even prefer to be termed "chairman" of a committee or a project—apparently they think that has more prestige. They consider suggestions like *chairwoman* to be a newfangled innovation. Yet the first use of *chairman* cited by the *Oxford English Dictionary* (*OED*) is in 1654 and the first use of *chairwoman* is 1699! *Chair* has been used alone since the seventeenth century. Indeed the *OED*'s first reference to *spokeswoman* is 1654! If we prefer something less cumbersome, we can call the person who speaks for a group its "representative."

The trend is also toward one designation for occupational descriptions; the use of -ess and -ix as suffixes is becoming obsolete. I cringe when I am introduced as an authoress. These endings are diminutives which diminish and trivialize; they tend to devalue women's work as though it were a hobby or avocation rather than real work. Women can also be poets, prophets, actors, administrators, executors.

## NAMING NAMES

There are other subtle ways of ignoring women's presence or diminishing their personhood. One is to speak of them only in terms of the men they are related to. For example, although most newspapers have given up the practice of referring to women by their husbands' names (Mrs. John R. Jones), religious magazines and church bulletins sometimes persist in it. Women always should be referred to by their own names, including their birth family names (Alice Jackson Jones). After all, a person's first name is indeed their baptismal or Christian name. While the birth family name is still commonly determined in this country by a person's father, using it for a married woman does allow her to retain a reference to her mother and to the name which was hers for at least the first decades of her life.

In subsequent references to people, we should also consistently use first names or last names, not last names for men and first names for women or people of other races or nationalities. The use of first names alone connotes familiarity. If one wishes to convey a feeling of friendship and community, first names are appropriate for everyone. On the other hand, in a more formal setting, the use of first names can connote lack of respect.

In regard to titles, one should use whatever the person prefers—forms should give multiple options such as Mr., Mrs., Ms., Miss, and Dr. A woman's marital status should not be given unless one knows she prefers that form. Thus the use of Ms.—which came initially not from rabid feminists of the nineteen-sixties but from secretarial manuals of the nineteen-forties—is appropriate for all women. In second references to individuals, again one should be consistent—Mr. Jensen and Ms. Phillips or Jensen and Phillips, not Jensen and Mrs. Phillips or Jensen and Rita.

*The Atlanta Journal and Constitution*, for example, in a story quoting Dr. Ruth Schmidt, president of Agnes Scott College, referred to her subsequently as simply "Ms. Schmidt," despite the fact that she has an earned doctorate in Spanish language and literature. Irate letter writers noted that the paper does not refer to Dr. James T. Laney, president of Emory University as Mr. Laney. They usually call him either Dr. Laney or President Laney, sometimes simply Laney.

We should show the same sensitivity when speaking or writing about historical examples: Katherine von Bora rather than Mrs. Luther or Martin Luther's wife. Many female saints are simply lost to us because no one ever bothered to record their Christian names—they are identified simply as someone's wife.

## DEALING WITH PRONOUNS

As we said in the beginning of this chapter, rather than using the masculine singular pronouns as though they were generic, many are returning to the earlier usage of Shakespeare, Milton, Bacon, and others, which allowed a collective such as *everyone* to be followed by the plural *their*.

The simplest solution is to recast the sentence or paragraph into the plural: "All members should bring their pledge cards to church next Sunday." In giving instructions, it is best to use the second person *you*, as in, "You should bring your pledge card." However, when I was teaching, I urged seminary students, when preaching, to use *we* and *us* because they had a tendency to use "you" and thus exclude themselves from discussions of sin and salvation, whereas in reality we are all in this predicament together. We should try to be consistent, though, and not shift back and forth between first, second, and third persons.

Sometimes, however, we want to accent the individual. We can use *he or she* and *her and his*, but this does become cumbersome. If we do use these, it is important not to put either pronoun first all the time. While *s/he* is sometimes used in writing, it loses its effectiveness in speaking. Even in writing the use of the slash (his/her, herself/himself) is very awkward. Another possibility is simply to alternate masculine and feminine pronouns, as in "A person must confess his sins, ask God to forgive her trespasses." This possibility retains the richness of gender-specific language with equity for both men and women. Another solution to the issue of pronouns is to use *one*: "One must offer oneself to God, rejoicing in one's salvation."

Again we usually do not need as many pronouns as we think we do. Recasting a sentence or a paragraph can often eliminate the dilemma entirely.

## THE WHOLE FAMILY OF GOD

In addition to monitoring our male-female language, we need to be more fully aware of the many other exclusions we perpetuate with our words.

A single parent recently told me about the frustration and anger she felt when she and her children participated in a weekend retreat her church sponsored to discuss sexuality in a Christian context. Every speaker talked as though every household contained a lovingly married couple and two children. Even single people on the church staff who worked with the youth programs felt compelled to support this illusion and keep quiet about their own sexuality—even though their struggles were probably closer to the teens' own present experience.

A blind friend alerted me to how often we use visual allusions and examples. We say, "As anyone can plainly see. . . ." or "God's handiwork is evident in the colors of the rainbow, the artistic design of a butterfly's wing." Jesus made it clear when he healed the blind man, that "it was not that this man sinned, or his parents, but that the works of God might be made manifest in him" (John 9:3), yet preachers and hymn-writers often persist (with the Twelve) in using the phrase "once I was blind but now I see" as a metaphor for sin and salvation. This is not to suggest again that we eliminate all visual images, but that we use a variety of sense images—hearing, smelling, touching, tasting—as well as those of seeing.

Even though we have renamed the "old folks' class" the "senior citizens' group," we still, as a culture, value youth and devalue old age. Many Asian cultures revere the experience and wisdom of those among them who have lived the longest.

In this country, however, some people throw "over-the-hill" parties for those turning forty or fifty! Black decorations and food usually set the theme—in itself a racist metaphor. In many Asian cultures, white is the color of mourning and death. Many Christian churches have discarded the black pall and vestments at funerals, not out of any sensitivity to Black Christians but in order to associate white with victory over death, triumph, and resurrection. This may not be a basic improvement, but it certainly illustrates the complexity of the issues!

About now you may be thinking, "If I try to be sensitive to all of these inclusive language issues, I'll never open my mouth again!"—particularly if you, like me, have a tendency toward foot-in-mouth disease anyway! I have found several things that will help us in our dilemma. First, we need to work on our own self-esteem. That may sound paradoxical and selfish, yet I think the reason most of us put down other people, consciously or unconsciously, is that we do not feel very good about ourselves. You may have seen or heard or read the affirmation, "God don't make no junk!" When we really begin to know in our guts that God created us, that we are made in God's image, that Christ died for us, and that God loves us individually and collectively with an everlasting love, then we can love and respect ourselves and others, even those who differ from us and with us.

Second, we need to be honest and humble and yet accepting of our own sins and shortcomings. When we have patience with ourselves, we can have patience with others. Every person is valued by God, and every person struggles and fails sometimes just as we do. For example, when we repress and deny our own sexual desires, it is easy to project sexual promiscuity and deviance on other groups—whether they be female (favorite targets of the early church "fathers") or Black or homosexual or of another class or whatever. When we acknowledge and accept our own sexuality, we find the sexuality of others more acceptable and understandable. As we are more empathic with ourselves, we become more empathic with others. When we feel more empathy with others, we speak of them more gently, more inclusively.

We also begin to take ourselves more seriously and less seriously. We can respect ourselves and laugh at ourselves. When we are secure in ourselves, we can be less defensive. When we give up the illusion that we are perfect—or the expectation that we should be perfect—we can acknowledge our mistakes, apologize, and continue to try to do better. When we do put both feet in our mouths, when we say something totally offensive and insensitive (and we will, no matter how carefully we try), we can acknowledge our mistake, say we are sorry, and try not to do it again. When a sister or brother points out our error, we can acknowledge our own hurt and shame and anger at being caught in our mistake and still respond with love to their hurt and anger. Thus we can begin to function truly as the body of Christ which Paul describes in 1 Corinthians 12, knowing that "if one member suffers, all suffer together; if one member is honored, all rejoice together" (vs. 26).

## DISCUSSION:

1. Using a chalkboard, overhead projector, or piece of newsprint, list ways in which language can be and has been used to value and devalue men and women (e.g., stud or brute, lady or hussy, etc.) Do the same for such groups as rich and poor, tall and short, those of different races, of different nations, homosexuals, the old and the young, those who are differently abled, those who lack education, or those with different levels of intelligence. With a larger group, you could divide into groups of three or four and assign each group to work on words concerning a particular set of people listed above. Have each group post its list of words on a wall or chalkboard.

2. How do you prefer to be referred to in print—in speaking? Can you think of examples of references to you that made you angry or happy?

3. How would you feel if you had to give up your name, or how did (do) you feel about having a "married" name that is different from the one you were born with?

4. What nicknames have you been given at various points in your life? How do you feel about them? What insights does this give you into how others may or do feel about various names they may be called?

# VI. Translating the Bible

*F*or at least a century and a half women have been well aware that Bible translators have short-changed them.

When Lucy Stone (1818–1893) was a little girl, she discovered Genesis 3:16: "Your desire shall be to thy husband, and he shall rule over thee " (KJV). That injunction depressed her so much that she went to her mother and asked what she could take to make herself die. When her mother found out what was tempting her daughter to suicide, she could only tell her that indeed the Bible did teach woman's submission. Rather than despairing, Stone resolved to learn Greek and Hebrew to "see how men had falsified the text," according to her daughter Alice Stone Blackwell (*Lucy Stone*, p. 16).

Eventually she went to Oberlin College, studied the original languages, and contended for the rest of her life that the Bible, rightly interpreted, supported women's rights. Blackwell tells the story of how once on a speaking tour Stone found herself sharing an Ohio riverboat with a minister who began to argue with her about women's headcoverings. Losing the argument, he told her she should study Scriptures more carefully. She told him, "I have studied them in their original. I have read them in Greek and can translate them for you" (p. 134). She went on to give him a lesson in the Greek words involved. It soon became clear that he knew no Greek and not that much about the English Bible.

Abolitionist Sarah Grimke (1792–1873), in her *Letters on the Equality of the Sexes and the Condition of Woman* (1837), began by declaring,

> I shall depend solely on the Bible to designate the sphere of woman, because I believe almost every thing that has been written on this subject, has been the result of a misconception of the simple truths revealed in the Scriptures, in consequence of the false translation of many passages of Holy Writ.

Like Stone, she determined to search the original languages because, as she said, it was inspired by God and "King James's translators certainly were not inspired!" (p. 4).

In the third letter she lodged a "protest against the false translation of some passages by the MEN who did that work, and against the perverted interpretation by the MEN who undertook to write commentaries thereon." She suggested that when women were "admitted to the honor of studying Greek and Hebrew," they would "produce some various readings of the Bible a little different from those we now have" (p. 16). And indeed they have done so.

## WORKING IN TRANSLATION

In thinking about the Bible, one must always keep clearly in mind the fact that we are reading from translations. We are two or three thousand years removed from the languages and cultures in which the texts were written. While our most recent translations are continually being enriched by such discoveries as the Dead Sea Scrolls and the Nag Hammadi texts, we are still unclear about the exact denotations of some words and certainly without a full understanding of the connotations and nuances of most words. Even when scholars have a fairly accurate fix on the meaning of a given Hebrew or Greek word, they may not be able to find a really good equivalent in English.

For example, many of us are familiar with the story of Jesus' disciples being criticized by the Pharisees for picking and eating food on the Sabbath. In Matthew 12 the King James translators say that as the disciples walked "through the corn," they began to "pluck the ears of corn, and to eat" (cf. Mark 2:23; Luke 6:1). We picture them strolling through a field in Iowa, stripping off a ripening cob, pulling back the husk and silk, to nibble on the tender kernels. But corn or maize is a plant native to the New World. No corn stalks tassled in first-century Palestine. Nor did many in King James' England in 1611. The British Corn Laws of the nineteenth century forbade the importation of all grains intended for consumption by human or beast, primarily wheat and oats. Thus the Revised Standard Version is more accurate, if less graphic, in saying the disciples plucked "heads of grain."

Recently English-speaking Christians have been blessed with numerous translations of the Bible—the Jerusalem Bible, the New English Bible, the New American Standard, the American Standard, the New International Version, the Good News Bible—plus several very popular if less academically accurate paraphrases—Ken Taylor's Living Bible, J. B. Phillips' version, Clarence Jordan's Cotton Patch Version of Luke and Acts. We of all people should be very aware of how translations by groups of equally dedicated and informed scholars can vary.

One obvious problem is that there is rarely an exact equivalent from one language to another. The Bible was originally written in Hebrew, Aramaic, and Greek. Jewish scholars translated the Old Testament into Greek; it was called the Septuagint (or LXX because tradition tells us it was done by about seventy scholars in roughly seventy days). Then Jerome, with help from Paula, Eustochium, Marcella, and the rest, translated the whole Bible from Greek into a Latin version called the Vulgate. Some English translations were done from the Septuagint and Vulgate. Now scholars go back to earlier Hebrew and Greek manuscripts, but we have none of the original writings and our earliest manuscripts sometimes show minor variations in their contents.

To communicate the meaning of one Greek word sometimes takes two or three in English. That is the point of the Amplified Bible. For example, the familiar John 3:16, "God so loved the world, that he gave his only begotten Son, that whosoever believeth in him should not perish, but have everlasting life" (KJV), becomes in the Amplified Version, "God so greatly loved *and* dearly prized the world that He [even] gave up His only begotten Son, so that whoever believes in [trusts, clings to, relies on] Him may not perish—come to destruction, be lost—but have eternal [everlasting] life."

Thus one has a choice in translating between choosing one English word which approximately translates one Greek or Hebrew word or choosing an English word, words, or phrase which best represents a "dynamic equivalence" to the Greek or Hebrew expression. We know that languages use not only nouns referring to objects but also idioms, particular words or phrases that refer to concepts and are unique to one language. If they are literally translated into another language, they will not convey the same meaning. To cite another biblical example, the King James translators sometimes refer to "feet" in the Old Testament rather than "private parts" (to use another euphemism). In 1 Samuel 24:3 they note that King Saul went into a cave "to cover his feet" and found David hiding there. The Revised Standard Version says more candidly that Saul went into the cave "to relieve himself" (another example of a euphemism or an idiom peculiar to English) an insight which gives added dimensions to the story of Ruth and Boaz at the threshing floor!

Different cultures also have quite different concepts. In the twentieth-century West, we are clear that we think with the brain in our head, though we are less clear about where our emotions reside (in our heart? in our gut?). People in biblical times thought they thought with their hearts and emoted from their bowels. Thus the writer of Proverbs counsels: "Bow down thine ear, and hear the words of the wise, and apply thine heart unto my knowledge" (22:17, KJV). The Revised Standard Version renders this in more contemporary idiom:

> Incline your ear, and hear the words of the wise,
>     and apply your mind to my knowledge.

Jesus said that "what comes out of the mouth proceeds from the heart [*kardia*]. . . . For out of the heart [*kardia*] come evil thoughts" (Matt. 15:18–19). Whenever the King James says that Jesus "had compassion" on a person or a group of people (cf. Matt. 9:36; 14:14; 18:27; 20:34; Mark 1:41; 6:34; Luke 7:13; 10:33), more recent translations use the more contemporary idiom "his heart was filled with pity." Yet the Greek more literally says that "his bowels yearned." We sometimes find it baffling or amusing to read in the Old Testament such phrases as "her bowels yearned upon her son" (1 Kings 3:26, KJV), though this is more literally accurate than the Revised Standard Version's "her heart yearned for her son." If you still have trouble grasping the problem, simply try to explain to a person from another culture, whose native language is not English, what we mean when we say, "He flew by the seat of his pants!"

## THE QUESTION OF ACCURACY

In speaking about the Bible then, one's first concern is always accuracy. But obviously that is not a precise concept. Accuracy can mean simply choosing a word which means roughly the same thing in English, or it can mean attempting to convey in English more precisely what the author meant and the first hearers and readers understood by what the author said. Dr. Bruce Metzger, chair of the Revised Standard Version translation committee, argues that a literal translation must reproduce what a passage *says*, not what it *means*. But this is not exactly a neat division, nor should we be willing to sacrifice meaning if we believe that the purpose of Scripture is to communicate God's word to us today.

As an evangelical I am committed to the inspiration and authority of Scripture. I believe that we must continually strive for the most accurate translation, the one which most faithfully represents the original text. Yet my commitment is not to some historical, antiquarian document, but to the living Word of God, ever relevant to changing cultures, changing human conditions. God does not want us simply to preserve a relic from the past. God wants to communicate through the Bible with each of us today. Thus while we strive for accurate translations, we must also be aware of what that translation is communicating to people today. This is part of the motivation for the *Inclusive Language Lectionary*. When confronted by several different yet accurate translation possibilities, we should opt for the one which is most felicitous to the most people.

Women and men of the nineteenth century were quite aware of several inaccuracies in the King James Version. For example, many of them note that Psalm 68:11—"The *Lord* gave the word: great *was* the company of those that published *it*—" should have included a reference to women. They quote Adam Clarke, who in his commentaries suggests it should read, "of the female preachers there was a great host." The Revised Standard Version still has, "The Lord gives the command; / great is the host of those who bore the tidings." But the New American Standard translates the second line, "And women who proclaim the *good* tidings are a great host."

## PHOEBE THE DEACON

They were also aware more than a hundred years ago that the King James translators had slighted Phoebe in Romans 16:1 when they called her "a servant of the church which is at Cenchrea." The New American Standard and the New International versions repeat the error. The New English suggests that she "holds office" in the congregation at Cenchrea, while the Revised Standard calls her "a deaconess." The Living Bible patronizingly calls her "a dear Christian woman from the town of Cenchrea"! But as A. J. Gordon, founder of Gordon-Conwell Theological Seminary, pointed out in 1894,

> the same word *diakonos*, here translated "servant," is rendered "minister" when applied to Paul and Apollos (1 Cor. 3:5), and "deacon" when used of other male officers of the Church (1

Tim. 3:10, 12, 13). Why discriminate against Phoebe simply because she is a woman? The word "servant"is correct for the general unofficial use of the term, as in Matt. 22:11; but if Phoebe were really a functionary of the Church, as we have a right to conclude, let her have the honor to which she is entitled. If "Phoebe, a minister of the Church at Cenchreæ," sounds too bold, let the word be transliterated, and read, "Phoebe, a deacon"—a *deacon*, too, without the insipid termination "ess". . . . "Phoebe, a *servant*,"might suggest to an ordinary reader nothing more than the modern church drudge, who prepares sandwiches and coffee for an ecclesiastical sociable. . . . "Phoebe, a deacon," suggests a useful co-laborer of Paul, "traveling about on missionary and other labors of love."

The prejudices of the translations are even clearer when one realizes that the word *diakonos* is not a rare one, but a term found twenty-one times in the New Testament. When applied to men, it is most often translated minister or transliterated as deacon and assumed to denote an office of church administration. The term *deaconess* did not come into use until about the sixth century, so to insert it in Scripture at this point is clearly anachronistic.

## THE GOSPEL FOR MEN ONLY

By using the allegedly generic masculine, translators have also made it difficult for women to hear themselves addressed by Scripture. For example, I recently received a mailing from a Christian organization which included on the envelope and letterhead the verse, "You [Christ] bought men for God of every race, language, people and nation. . . " (Rev. 5:9). The insult to women is totally gratuitous because the phrase does not conform to any translation I have been able to find, and the word *men* does not appear in the Greek at all, a fact which the New American Standard Version makes clear by the use of italics. The Revised Standard Version, New English Bible, and New International Version all insert *men* without indicating that it is not in the original text, but even the Good News Bible and the Living Bible use "people" in this verse! The King James says, "for thou wast slain, and hast redeemed us to God by thy blood out of every kindred, and tongue, and people, and nation." Despite its faults, the King James is sometimes less sexist than more recent translations.

This is but one example of how many texts of Scripture are made to appear much more male-oriented than they are in the Greek and Hebrew. Citations for the term *man* take up twenty-two columns on the huge pages of my *Strong's Exhaustive Concordance*, and citations of *men* cover another fourteen columns. Each column includes 116 citations. This means that a woman reading an English Bible finds the words *man* or *men* more than four thousand times!

In Greek, however, the writers carefully made a distinction between *anthropos*, which means human, person, people, humanity, and *aner*, which means adult male and/or husband (the stem of *aner* is *andri-* and thus our words *androcentric* and *androgynous*). Like the word *gyne*, which means adult female and/or wife, one has no indication other than conjecture from context whether *aner* and *gyne* are referring to men and women in general or to married persons in particular—an extremely important distinction in trying to understand and apply a number of New Testament texts (another pair of words, *arsen* and *thelu*, male and female, are used only in Matt. 19:4; Rom. 1:26–27; and Gal. 3:28). That problem aside, the New Testament authors used *anthropos* predominantly. As Chapter 3 on Jesus notes, they almost always used the more generic term when speaking of Jesus, God Incarnate. They were also careful to use *anthropos* when speaking about people in general, a fact that is lost on English readers because translators have invariably rendered it "man" and "men."

Thus, for example, in the Revised Standard Version Titus 2:11 declares that "the grace of God has appeared for the salvation of all men," and 1 Timothy 2:4 says that God "desires all men to be saved" and goes on to say in 4:10 that "we have our hope set on the living, who is the Savior of all men." Frankly, that God does not offer much hope for me as a woman! But actually all of these verses in Greek have some form of the word *anthropos* and should read people.

On the other hand, we have sometimes unconsciously corrected the translators ourselves. A most notable and appropriate example is the Golden Rule, "Do unto others as you would have them do unto you." Both Matthew 7:12 and Luke 6:31 read roughly "whatsoever ye would that men should do to you, do ye even so to them" in the King James and "as you wish that men would do to you, do so to them" in the Revised Standard. The word *anthropos* appears in the Greek. Yet over the years, people have simply adopted a more inclusive phrasing for themselves.

In Hebrew a similar distinction is made between *'adam*, which means human being, *enosh*, which means a mortal, and *ish*, which means a male person. When the writers specifically wish to designate a female person, they use the word *'ishshah* or the plural *nashim*. Thus, for example, Proverbs 3:13 in the Revised Standard Version reads,

> Happy is the man who finds wisdom,
> and the man who gets understanding,

yet the text both times says *adam*, the person. We have been led to think of Adam as a proper name only, but it is actually a more general word. Old Testament scholar Phyllis Trible argues that the word, a play on the word for earth, should be translated the "earth creature" in Genesis 2:4–22, since the concept of sexual differentiation is not introduced until verse 23 when the words *'ish* and *'ishshah* are used (*God and the Rhetoric of Sexuality*, p.77). The Revised Standard Version translation committee has already admitted  that if these distinctions were observed two hundred male references in the Psalms alone could be eliminated.

In addition to translations of the terms above, the words *man* and *men* creep into the texts in at least two circumstances when there is no underlying Greek or Hebrew word. Matthew 10:41 illustrates the problem. In the Revised Standard Version it reads, "He who receives a prophet because he is a prophet shall receive a prophet's reward, and he who receives a righteous man because he is a righteous man shall receive a righteous man's reward." No word for man appears in the Greek though *man* appears three times in the English, and not once does the translator indicate that it is added. The verse begins with the pronoun *ho*, which a standard interlinear text indicates should be translated "one." Just as *prophet* is a noun in English without indication of gender, so the word *righteous* stands alone in Greek and could just as easily be translated "righteous one" in English since we do not ordinarily use "righteous" alone as a noun in the singular, though we do in the plural (e.g., "The souls of the righteous are in the hand of God," Wisdom 3:1). Usually in the New Testament, English references to a good man, rich man, or wise man have no male word behind them. In the texts they are simply adjectives with masculine noun endings and could just as accurately be translated as a good, rich, or wise person, or in the plural, simply the good, the rich, or the wise.

The Greek also frequently uses a pronoun, *tis*. The most abused text in this regard is 2 Corinthians 5:17 where the King James has, "Therefore if any man *be* in Christ, *he is* a new creature: old things are passed away; behold all things are become new." At least the translation indicates with italics that the pronoun *he* is a translator's addition. The word translated "man" is not a noun, but the pronoun *tis*. More accurate is the Revised Standard's, "Therefore, if any one is in Christ, he is a new creation," but the verse could very accurately be translated "anyone who is in Christ is a new creation," thus eliminating both sexist references. For other instances of the use of *tis*, compare translations of such verses as Luke 9:57; John 6:50; 15:6; 2 Corinthians 11:20; Hebrews 10:28; James 2:14; 2 Peter 2:19; and Revelation 3:20. In many cases the King James uses "whosoever." In some more recent translations, such clauses have been changed to begin "if a man. . . ."

If translators would conscientiously observe these distinctions in the original languages, they could eliminate at least half and probably many more male references which were obviously not intended by the original writers.

## *BROTHERS ALL ARE WE?*

Another translation which alienates women who are sensitive to the issue is the frequent reference in the Epistles to "brethren." For example, rather ironically in Galatians 1:11 Paul declares, "For I would have you know, brethren, that the gospel which was preached by me is not man's gospel!" Perhaps it wasn't, but one wouldn't know that from most English translations. The word, of course, is *anthropos* and should be understood to mean "human gospel" in contrast to divine revelation, but anyway, Paul still appears to be talking only to men, to his "brethren."

In Greek, however, the word translated "brethren" is *adelphoi*, which in English we would call a collective plural. Just as we use the Latin masculine plural *alumni* to speak of the graduates of a coeducational college, the Greeks used the masculine plural endings on collective nouns. The same word with a slightly different ending would have been used of a group of women. Indeed it appears from some New Testament examples that if one wished to apply *adelphoi* specifically to one gender or the other, one had to couple it with a gender noun. For some reason the major speeches by Peter and Paul in Acts are addressed to "men brothers," *andres adelphoi* (cf. Acts 2:29, 37; 7:2; 13:15, 26, 38; 15:7, 14; 22:1; 23:1, 6). On the other hand, Paul asks if he too does not have the right like other Apostles to be accompanied by a "sister woman," *adelphen gynaika* (1 Cor. 9:5). Thus those congregations to whom Paul's letters were first read all heard themselves addressed, not just the men.

To accurately translate the word into English one needs to use the phrase *sisters and brothers* since these equivalents are gender specific— unless one prefers *siblings*. A one-word translation which would convey the affection, if not the exact relationship, is *friends*. Interestingly, the Epistles of Peter and John in the same context use the word for beloved, *agapetoi* (cf. 1 Peter 2:11; 1 John 2:7).

The Bible occasionally also uses the word transliterated *philadelphia*, brotherly love. Again this should be translated "love for all brothers and sisters" or simply "the love of the community" because the authors were speaking of that mutual respect and reciprocity that characterized the early Christian community.

Just as women sometimes find it difficult to feel included when they are addressed as brethren, so too they find it a bit alien to be called sons of God. As a woman who has two brothers, I have always found it obvious that they are sons and brothers and I am neither. The Bible does often speak of sons, *huios*, but sometimes it does not have only males in mind. Sometimes the original texts use the Greek words *paidon* and *teknon*, which should more properly be translated "child" in the singular and "children" in the plural (for examples compare translations of John 1:12; Acts 3:13; 13:10; Phil. 2:15; 1 John 3:1–2). No translation indicates that in the parable in Matthew 21:28, Jesus really said, "A person had two children. . . ."

## HEAD

Many newer translations have read into Scripture and thus into their purported "translations" a much harsher view of women than the actual texts suggest. Most obvious in that regard is the treatment of Ephesians 5:22. Of course the sense of the passage begins with a discussion of Christian behavior in 5:1, and the immediate topic begins in 5:21, which many recent versions obscure by beginning a new paragraph at verse 22. But 5:21–23 says in the King James Version: "Submitting yourselves one to another in the fear of God. Wives, submit yourselves unto your own husbands, as unto the Lord. For the husband is the head of the wife, even as Christ is the head of the church: and he is the savior of the body." In the Greek the word *submit* does not appear in verse 22, which is a dependent clause reading literally "wives to their own husbands."

The word for head is *kephale*, which means very simply the round appendage atop a person's body. Paul uses the image repeatedly in Romans, 1 Corinthians, Ephesians, and Colossians to talk about the church's unity in Christ, with whom we are one body, one living organism. Paul reinforces the point in Ephesians 5:32 where he again points out that he is talking about Christ and the church and using marriage as an illustration, rather than the other way around.

The Revised Standard and New American Standard substitute "be subject" for submit, and unlike the King James and Revised Standard, the New American Standard uses italics to indicate that the phrase is introduced into verse 22 by the translators. The concept of mutual submission among believers, the body of Christ, is a common refrain in the Epistles, based on Jesus' injunction to "love one another as I have loved you" (John 15:12). In Romans 12:10, for example, Paul bids everyone to love one another with *philadelphia*, sibling affection, to "outdo one another in showing honor." In 1 Corinthians 12:26, using the same image of the body, Paul notes that "if one member suffers, all suffer together; if one member is honored, all rejoice together." In Philippians 2:3–4, Christians are instructed to "do nothing from selfishness or conceit, but in humility count others better than yourselves. Let each of you look not only to his own interests, but also the interests of others."

Ken Taylor in his paraphrased Living Bible reads his own interpretation into Ephesians 5:21–23: "Honor Christ by submitting to each other. You wives must submit to your husbands' leadership in the same way you submit to the Lord. For a husband is in charge of his wife in the same way Christ is in charge of his body the church." Suddenly the simple word "head" has been transformed into concepts of "leadership" and being "in charge."

Similarly the Good News Bible, which originally advertised that it would have a simpler vocabulary so that it could be read by those with less education, transforms a simple, familiar four-letter common noun into a nine-letter concept. Verse 23 reads, "For a husband has authority over his wife just as Christ has authority over the church." Actually if one simply continues to read the passage, it is clear that Christ's relationship to the church is not based on "authority" but on self-giving.

The various versions do similar surgery on 1 Corinthians 11:3, which in the King James Version says, "But I would have you know, that the head of every man is Christ; and the head of the woman *is* the man; and the head of Christ *is* God."Taylor goes so far here as to rearrange the order in attempt to use this verse to support a vertical hierarchy, a great chain of being. According to the Living Bible, "a wife is responsible to her husband, her husband is responsible to Christ, and Christ is responsible to God." The Good News Bible retains the original order, but says that "Christ is supreme over man, the husband is supreme over his wife, and God is supreme over Christ." Never mind that the church declared a subordinationist view of the Trinity heretical in the fourth century!

As we noted previously, people in New Testament times did not consider the head the place where decisions were made. Thus to say that the Bible teaches that the husband is the head of the house (a common misreading of this passage) and that he is the leader, ordained by God to make all decisions for the family, is totally anachronistic, to say nothing of contrary to the rest of New Testament teaching about how Christians are to behave with each other. A study of the concept of head and body in the Epistles, a common metaphor not primarily connected with marriage, shows that the writers use the image of a human person, a living organism, to speak of the unity of believers and the way spouses and all Christians are parts of a living, harmonious whole, which grows through mutual submission and support.

## WOMEN IN AUTHORITY

Allegedly objective and literal translations have also been used to deny women authority in the church. In the same 1 Corinthians 11 passage, verse 10 reads rather literally, "Because of this, a woman ought to have authority upon the head because of the angels." Many Bible scholars believe the "authority upon the head"was some emblem of the fact that the church had recognized this person as a prophet. There is absolutely no reference to veils or headcoverings nor to men or marriage, yet the Good News Bible here reads, "On account of the angels, then, a woman should have a covering over her head to show that she is under her husband's authority." Likewise the Living Bible declares, "So a woman should wear a covering on her head as a sign that she is under man's authority, a fact for all the angels to notice and rejoice in." In this instance the King James comes closest: "For this cause ought the woman to have power on *her* head because of the angels." Paul did not explain what he meant by the remark about the angels, nor have scholars since that time figured out what he meant.

Similarly, 1 Corinthians 14:34 has been used to silence women in the church. It does read, "Women should remain silent in the churches. They are not allowed to speak, but must be in submission, as the Law says" (NIV). This New International Version reading is correct except in the capitalization of "Law," which implies that the Old Testament somewhere prohibits women's speaking or commands their submission, which it does not. Again the Living Bible goes far beyond accuracy in saying, "Women should be silent during the church meetings. They are not to take part in the discussion, for they are subordinate to men as the Scriptures also declare." The Good News Bible makes similar assumptions in amplifying it to read, "The women should keep quiet in the meetings. They are not allowed to speak; as the Jewish Law says, they must not be in charge." However, read literally in context, the passage suggests that women should behave respectfully in church, not "chattering" but listening with a worshipful demeanor. Only patriarchal presumption has led to its use to prohibit women's leadership in local congregations.

Another translation bias has obscured the example of women in church leadership. Many churches believe that only men can be "elders" within the church; in some congregations the word *elder* is applied to men only and is contrasted with *deaconesses* for the female group. The men serve communion and participate in the administration of church affairs while the women are restricted to charitable activities and preparation of the communion (and washing the dishes afterward!). However, the passage in Scripture which describes the office of elder is 1 Timothy 5:17 and following. The word for elders is *presbuteroi.*

Nothing in the passage indicates that it refers to men only. Verse 22 in the King James does say, "Lay hands suddenly on no man, neither be partaker of other men's sins: keep thyself pure," but there are no words meaning "man"or "men's" in the original. It says "no one" and simply "others." The chapter opens with a discussion of *presbutero* and *presbuteras*—an older man and older women. The word is the same. It could just as accurately be translated a male elder and female elders. Titus 2:2–3 uses similar terms, *presbutas* and *presbutidas*.

Such examples make it evident that translators have manipulated Scripture to discriminate against women and to buttress male dominance. They also show, contrary to the protestations of some biblical scholars, that much could be done to make the language of the Bible much more inclusive without impairing in the least the accuracy of the translation. Indeed the use of such inclusive language would more closely approximate the intentions of the original authors. We who say that we revere the sacred texts must be careful that we are truly respecting the text and not simply clinging to traditional verbal formulas for our own prejudices. Many have argued for the retention of the King James Version simply because its familiarity makes it seem more poetic. While its familiar cadences do have a majestic ring, most people now realize that the discovery of numerous manuscripts since 1611 has given scholars the ability to produce a much more accurate text. Just as our knowledge of the original languages has increased, so the English we speak has changed. The process of transmitting the ancient messages into the living language of any people is an ongoing task. But if we contend that the Bible is the very Word of God, then we must continue that task if we are to be faithful to God.

## RIGHTLY DIVIDING THE WORD OF GOD

So how can the average layperson sort out these issues? While the problem sounds as though it requires seminary courses in Greek and Hebrew, it does not. A few simple-to-use reference books clarify these issues for anyone who wants to look.

First of all, compare translations of various passages. One can easily acquire a library of different versions of the Bible in hardback or paperback by shopping at used book stores, rummage sales, or book sales such as those promoted by the American Association of University Women or Brandeis University. Magazine articles are readily available to clarify the strengths and weaknesses of various translations. The Revised Standard Version is usually considered the norm. The New International Version is quite close to the literal sense of the words, though it is not sensitive to the issues we have been discussing. Trust committee versions more (KJV, RSV, NIV, JB, NASV, etc.); beware of those versions essentially compiled by one person (Living Bible, Phillips). Committee versions tend to strive for a more faithful rendering of the text while an individual person usually tends to convey personal interpretations.

Many homes already have a *Strong's Exhaustive Concordance*. This is a valuable reference book which indexes every word used in the King James Version. Many people never notice the numbers to the right of every entry, but these indicate the Hebrew or Greek word used. In the back of the volume are Hebrew and Greek dictionaries of sorts. For example, by looking at the number and then finding it in the back, you can tell whether a certain New Testament verse which says *man* really contains *aner, anthropos,* or merely *tis*. For example, a mere comparison of numbers makes it instantly obvious that the word translated "silence" when applied to women in 1 Timothy 2:11 is the same word translated "quietness" when applied to men in 2 Thessalonians 3:12.

Another way to get the same information for the New Testament is to use an interlinear text. This is a book which has an English translation in the left-hand column of each page (either KJV or RSV are available) and the Greek text with a literal English equivalent underneath each word in the right-hand column. Again it is easy to see what word is used even without learning the Greek alphabet, simply by comparing the characters. You will soon pick up the Greek alphabet too in the process. Interlinear texts are also available for the Old Testament. If you get intrigued by the language, you can go on with teach-yourself books on Hebrew and New Testament Greek or the textbooks used in seminary language classes.

Certainly this process does not provide a sophisticated knowledge of the original languages, but you can gain basic insights into the issues. This is the way I have compiled most of the information in this chapter. Bible dictionaries, lexicons, and other reference books found in libraries can offer further help. The information is within the reach of any layperson who wants to dig for it.

## DISCUSSION:

1. How do you feel when you read or hear read in church Scripture passages using such phrases as "salvation for all men" and "if any man be in Christ, he is a new creation"?

2. Does it bother you to be called "brethren"? What are some contemporary words which would convey what the New Testament writers meant when they used this? How would you like to have your pastor address your congregation?

3. What do you do in your own Bible study to get at the real meaning of various Scripture passages? What reference books do you personally own or does your church library have to help you prepare Bible studies, Sunday school lessons, and other programs?

4. Pick a passage such as Ephesians 5:21–33 or 1 Corinthians 11:3–16 and compare them in as many translations as you can find. How do they differ? How are they similar? What do you learn about these various translations from your study? Compare your conclusions with an article or articles comparing the strengths and weaknesses of various translations (e.g., Berkeley and Alvera Mickelsen, "Does Male Dominance Tarnish Our Translations?" *Christianity Today*, 5 October 1979, pp. 23–27).

# VII. Praise God!

*A*ll of the concerns of this book are particularly important in the services of the church in which we join in the worship of God, proclaiming our faith to other Christians and to those who come seeking to know God.

Many women can recount tales of the Sunday morning they walked into church and were immediately asked to join in singing the hymn "Rise Up, O Men of God." One of my most vivid memories is of an intimate communion service during which the minister twice addressed the congregation as "my brothers" when it consisted entirely of six women. Also poignant is the recollection of the service supposedly to celebrate the memory of a female saint in which the minister elected to begin the readings with the famous passage from Ecclesiasticus, "Let us now praise famous men . . ." (44:1)—this again to a congregation composed entirely of women.

On a more positive note, I experience healing personally every time my current minister revises the language of a small Wednesday morning healing service for its usual congregation of women. He begins the prayers with a plea to "God the Father, whose will is health and salvation for all humankind" (rather than "mankind"). Later he prays to "Almighty God, giver of life and health, who sent your only Son into the world to make people whole." The text reads, "to make men whole."

For at least a century Christians, male and female, have been observing that the ratio of women to men in most church services is two to one. Sociologists and quantitative historians researching the exact figures are finding that observation accurate. Thus the use of male language excludes roughly two-thirds of any given congregation from the most meaningful participation.

In addition, noninclusive language also offers a distorted gospel to Christians and those wanting to become Christians. It conveys the message that the Christian faith is for men only or at least for men primarily. It does not say what God and Scripture say: that the God who created us loves us every one and offers all of us salvation and wholeness. As Thomas and Sharon Neufer Emswiler argue so cogently in their book *Wholeness in Worship*,

> The inner dynamic of shalom is outward in concern for the world. Once the truth of shalom touches us, we know that this truth can only find fulfillment as all people are included. . . .
>
> The same driving force is present in wholistic worship. It is not satisfied until all are one in God. Excluding people because of their age, race, cultural background, physical or mental handicaps, or religious tradition is a denial of shalom and precludes wholeness in worship. The same is true of more subtle exclusions in worship such as the use of sexist language and overemphasizing the mind at the expense of the body. Wholistic worship also insists on the valuing of all our times, past, present, and future. . . . Wholeness in worship moves us toward social commitment. We celebrate our journey toward personal fulfillment but recognize that this journey is inevitably thwarted unless we also move toward social fulfillment. (p. 3)

True worship and true service are inclusive; their goal is *shalom*, salvation, wholeness for ourselves and our world.

In the worship of God, our goal should be not to eliminate certain images of God but to present a variety of images so that every person present can relate to God more deeply for having been in the service. The goal is not to exclude but to include as much and as many as possible.

## SCRIPTURE

Throughout this book we have looked at the resources of Scripture. In terms of worship, several distinctions should be kept in mind. The purpose of using Scripture in worship is to draw the worshipers closer to God and to proclaim the essence of the faith to those who do not know it.

Thus in worship one handles Scripture a bit differently than in, say, a classroom or Bible study setting. In teaching and study one normally uses several different translations to find the one which seems most accurate or relevant. Usually a class also studies whole books in sequence or various topics throughout the Bible. In worship one takes Scripture passages out of their original contexts and groups them together (the lectionary contains readings from the Old Testament, the Epistles, the Psalms, and the Gospels for each service) according to the progression of the church year from Advent to Pentecost for use in the congregational context. Thus in worship the language of Scripture should be made as inclusive as possible so that people will not be distracted and alienated by gender references. Here Scripture is not intended as a source to be studied, analyzed, and dissected, but as an *aid* to worship and as a vehicle for proclamation of God's love and concern.

The *Inclusive Language Lectionary*, based on the three-year cycle of readings jointly agreed upon by Roman Catholics and the major Protestant denominations, is intended for precisely this purpose. If, however, a given congregation would find its choice of language too much of a departure from traditional phrases, the *Lectionary* can still be used by pastors and worship leaders as a personal tool to alert them to places where language needs to be and can be made more inclusive. Another alternative lectionary is *Hearing the Word: An Inclusive Language Liturgical Lectionary*, published by St. Stephen and the Incarnation Church in Washington, D.C.

In my own study I have marked one particular Bible

which I happened to be reading devotionally when I became interested in this topic. Comparing the text with a Greek interlinear, I used a code to indicate whether the Greek had *anthropos*, or *aner* next to each use of man or men. If it had neither, I put a diagonal line through the word, indicating that there was no basis for inserting a male reference there. Now when I am asked to read a particular Scripture I can glance at that text and spot any changes which may need to be made and their basis in the Greek, without having to go back to the Greek text itself. One could also use a highlighter pen to mark an interlinear or Greek New Testament.

In many churches the people in the pews do not follow the reading word-for-word in their own Bibles. They listen to the reading. Even in congregations where everyone brings Bibles and follows the reading, they now have a variety of translations. After careful preparation—consulting different translations, the *Inclusive Language Lectionary*, and even a Greek or Hebrew text—the worship leader should be able to make at least a few changes of men to people and brethren to brothers and sisters without most people in the congregation even noticing. Most of those who do notice will feel the warmth of inclusion.

Phrases of Scripture used out of context as calls to worship, affirmations of forgiveness, and benedictions can be similarly altered. They can also be varied. Many congregations get into a rut. My father, though upset by my becoming an Episcopalian, once commented that his own Christian and Missionary Alliance Church had just as rigid an order of service with their weekly bulletins as the Episcopalians did with their *Book of Common Prayer*. Those churches which pride themselves on their freedom of worship often find themselves using the same words week after week. (One of my personal favorites was "here we raise our Ebenezer for hitherto has the Lord helped us," uttered every Sunday by a pastor in his pastoral prayer. After I explained to my mother the image the phrase evoked for me, we both had to smother giggles.) Even those who follow more formal books of worship have alternatives. One can choose to use more inclusive alternatives from among those given, or one can dig into Scripture to find the inclusive ones which are available there.

A number of resources are available for inclusive language worship texts and for help in constructing one's own liturgies (see the "Resources" at the end of this book).

## PRAYER

The contrasting styles of prayer were best illustrated for me at the worship service for the installation for Dr. Ruth Schmidt as president of Agnes Scott College, Decatur, Georgia. The man who gave the opening prayer referred to God as Father exclusively and repeatedly. The woman who gave a later prayer carefully selected a variety of addresses for God, each one suitable to the subject for which she was praying at that point. Go and do thou likewise!

Those who would lead others in public prayer should immerse themselves in the Psalms and in the beautiful prayers left us by the saints of the past. Both remind us of myriad ways in which we can address God. Another function of the Psalms and great prayers of the past is that they lift us beyond our own often petty concerns into more universal concerns and into the contemplation and adoration of God.

One of the ancient forms of prayer which I have found most helpful is the "Jesus Prayer," popularized in Western Christianity by the Russian Orthodox nineteenth-century spiritual classic *The Way of the Pilgrim*. The traditional formulation, to be said repeatedly until it becomes prayer without ceasing, is, "Lord Jesus Christ, have mercy on me." A longer version suggested is, "Lord Jesus Christ, Son of God, have mercy on me, a sinner." In my own devotion I have chosen to phrase it, "Lord Jesus Christ, Lamb of God, have mercy."

We can also meditate on creative ways in which we might wish to address God. I will never forget the prayer which Sister Margaret Ellen Traxler prayed at an ecumenical gathering which included many Jewish women. She began, "Our Loved One...." I have often emulated her example by beginning,

"Beloved God. . . ."

Benedictions, likewise, need not always have the traditional trinitarian formula of "Father, Son, and Holy Ghost." Some favor the formulation "Creator, Redeemer, and Sanctifying Spirit" or "Maker, Savior, and Sustainer." Others object that this speaks of God's activity rather than the persons of the Trinity. So instead we might use "In the name of God, Yahweh, Jesus, and the Holy Spirit" or "God, Jehovah, Jesus, and the Holy Spirit," or "God, the Great I Am, Jesus the Christ, and the Spirit of Life." Fourteenth-century mystic Julian of Norwich meditated for years on the Trinity, filling the longer version of her *Showings* or *Revelations of Divine Love* with numerous formulations: "God is the Creator and the protector and the lover" (p. 183); God is "almighty, all wise and all good" (p.184); "And so in our making, God almighty is our loving Father, and God all wisdom is our loving Mother, with the love and the goodness of the Holy Spirit, which is all one God, one Lord" (p. 293). We can certainly adapt one of her formulations or allow the Spirit to speak through her and inspire in us new formulations for our day.

A number of creative revisions of the Doxology have been offered. Perhaps the simplest is to repeat "Praise God" in the first three lines (rather than using "Praise him . . ." in the second and third lines), and then substitute "Praise Christ, Creator, Holy Ghost" in the final line. Although this reverses the order of the first two titles, it fits the melody.

Some have argued cogently that all ministers should retain the traditional baptismal formula—"I baptize you in the name of the Father, Son, and Holy Spirit"—because this is the one common element of the sacrament that is recognized by most Christian churches. I have been told, however, that William Sloan Coffin, pastor of Riverside Church in New York City, sometimes uses the formula: "In the name of the Father, Son, and Holy Spirit, the God and Mother of us all."

Again the goal in prayer is not to eliminate any given form entirely, but to enrich our prayer life, corporately and personally. There is always a danger of confusing our own personal preferences with theological verities. Just because I find a given form of address in prayer most meaningful and moving is no sign that it is either the most theologically appropriate or at all meaningful to you, and vice versa. Just as God speaks to us through natural phenomena, biblical images, the visions of prophets and mystics, and the imaginative images of great writers, so we can speak back to God using images from these sources and from the resonances of our own souls.

## PROCLAMATION

While Scripture texts, worship liturgies, and hymns are often preprinted and thus difficult to change, the proclamation of the word is the responsibility of the preacher, so it leaves no excuse for not using inclusive language.

*The Liberating Word*, edited by Letty Russell, offers a number of helpful suggestions for interpreting Scripture in new ways which amplify women's participation. First, try to read each passage as though it were the first time, without preconceptions. Looking at different translations helps here. Second, try to retell the story from a woman's point of view. Third, ask what is omitted as well as what is included. For example, why does Jesus tell the ten lepers to go show themselves to the priests (Luke 17:14) but not the woman with the issue of blood (Luke 8:43–48)? Fourth, always study the text within its context and beware of any point based on a single phrase or verse. Fifth, check out the cultural, historical, and literary settings. We always first interpret Scripture from our own cultural understandings, but this can be very misleading in interpreting documents from other cultures. Sixth, remember that Scripture originated in and has been passed down by patriarchal cultures. Thus the texts often reflect androcentric situations, conditions, and values. So do standard reference works with which you might supplement your own study. Thus you must finally bring a feminist perspective to your reading and proclamation of Scripture. New Testament scholar Elisabeth Schüssler Fiorenza calls it a "hermeneutics of suspicion" (*In Memory of Her*, p. 56). We must give priority to texts which offer salvation equally to men and women, which call all people to their rightful wholeness in the body of Christ.

One should be very careful about assumptions regarding male-female relationships in Scripture. For example, it is often glibly assumed that all of the apostles were men. If one means by *apostle* the Twelve, then they were all men. But Paul called himself an apostle and defined the term as one who had seen the risen Lord (1 Corinthians 15:3–10). The first person to see the risen Lord by all Gospel accounts was Mary Magdalene (John 20:11–18); it was she who informed the Twelve. Other women disciples, among them women who had followed Jesus all the way from the beginning of his ministry in Galilee, also saw Jesus after the resurrection. Romans 16:7 speaks of Junia as one "of note among the apostles" (although the Revised Standard obscures this by calling her and Andronicus, who may have been her husband, "kinsmen" and inserts the word "man" into the text where there is no word for "men"). Fourth-century theologian and preacher Chrysostom spoke of her as a woman apostle. I also once heard a preacher try to explain his lack of references to women in a sermon about being disciples by saying that "in that culture" women were not disciples because women were not free to travel about with Jesus. He would not even have had to research the cultural background if he had paid attention to passages such as Luke 8:2–3 and the Passion narratives which make it clear that at least one group of women had followed Jesus every step of the way from Galilee.

Going beyond Scripture in proclamation, a preacher should be careful to use both women and men as examples from Scripture, history, and contemporary life. Mention Abraham and Sarah, Priscilla and Aquila, Mary and Martha, Miriam and Moses, the woman who anointed Jesus' head as well as the little boy who offered his lunch of loaves and fishes.

From history we have innumerable examples of women to supplement the familiar men—Augustine, Aquinas, Luther, Calvin, Wesley, Barth. Worship public and private would be greatly enriched by the mystics. The classical treatment of the subject is Evelyn Underhill's *Mysticism*. In it she offers an explanation of the phenomenon along with examples from such women as Julian of Norwich, Catherine of Sienna, Mechthild of Magdeburg, Madame Guyon, along with such men as Walter Hilton, Bernard of Clairvaux, and Jakob Boehme. Then there are the lives of the saints from such early figures as Monica, Melania, and Macrina to the early Quakers, Wesley's women preachers, and America's pioneer missionaries. I have told some of their stories in *Great Women of Faith*. Other anthologies such as Edith Deen's *Great Women of the Christian Faith* and Mary L. Hammack's *Dictionary of Women in Church History* offer many more. One can also draw on the lives of women hymnwriters for illustration.

When choosing contemporary illustrations, we should be careful to speak of men and women; girls and boys; older and younger people; people of color; married and single; rich, poor, and middle class; handicapped; Western World and Third World. In doing so, we also need to avoid stereotypes such as a male banker and a female secretary. We need to use illustrations to which different members of the congregation can relate, yet we must avoid suggesting that only men understand how automobiles work and only women understand how to bake bread. On the other hand, we should also avoid any hint of "Wow! isn't that unusual!" when referring to someone who does something contrary to the usual stereotypes. We must be very wary about any example which is condescending to women, children, the handicapped, single people, homosexuals, or those of other races and ethnic groups. Usually this problem goes beyond specific examples and betrays a condescending attitude in general. A person who has a basic respect for themselves and for others as God's creations and the objects of God's love will not use examples which gain their pungency at anyone else's expense.

We should not assume that everything is masculine either. One speaker began with a story about two hunters in Alaska who came across the footprints of a grizzly bear. Said one to the other, "Why don't you go that way and see where he went. I'll go this way and see where he came from!" Why not assume it was a she-bear?

Our culture also often projects other dualisms onto male and female—mind and body, intellect and emotion, reason and feeling, logic and intuition, strength and beauty, activity and passivity, realism and optimism. Such writers as Rosemary Radford Ruether and Anne Wilson Schaef have explained at length the destructive nature of dualism (*Sexism and God-Talk,* 160ff; *Women's Reality,* pp. 147–159). Wholeness for every person involves both poles and all that lies between; true proclamation of the gospel thus contains the same. Our Christian faith is a belief system and a personal experience and an ongoing life-process.

## HYMNS

The most difficult aspect of worship to make inclusive is music, mainly because we are more rigidly tied to written texts and these texts are matched to music by rhyme and meter. *Man* and *men* are attractive and hard to replace in this context because they have only one syllable. *Person* and *people* have two. Changing the sexist language in a hymn often requires major surgery, and that means printing all the words in the bulletin or on a song sheet, which becomes very complicated. So what are the alternatives?

If you are totally tied to a given hymnal, you can at least very consciously choose a variety of hymns for a given service. If one offends, then another may soothe. I once went through a hymnal and circled every male reference in the hymns with one color felt-tipped pen and every positive reference to females or feminine images in another color. Then I could tell at a glance which hymns on a given topic or for a given liturgical season were more inclusive.

The point of worship is to communicate with our God; thus we will want to balance those hymns that speak *about* God with those that speak *to* God. Thus we might choose hymns like "Break Thou the Bread of Life," "Jesus, Keep Me Near the Cross," or "O God, Our Help in Ages Past" rather than or along with "His Banner Over Me Is Love." Here again sometimes "older is better." The Puritans used nothing but the Psalms. The most recent hymns, particularly those written in the past one hundred and thirty years are the most sexist; the more ancient hymns, more inclusive.

If a hymn has only one or two masculine references, one can suggest to the congregation in the bulletin and/or orally before the music begins that they can substitute more inclusive language such as *one* for *he*.

However, many congregations now use a variety of song books, print texts in their bulletins, or even use an overhead projector to introduce new music. In these situations it is easier to choose inclusive language texts or to modify existing ones.

Many contemporary religious songs use gender-specific pronouns without ever explaining them, making the music indistinguishable from secular music. Once when I was visiting the church in which I was reared, we began the service by singing "He Is Lord." "He" was never identified by name. It reminded me of the John Lennon song "My Sweet Lord," a hymn to the Hindu god, Krishna. Then a couple sang a duet titled "Depend On Me." The man told us beforehand that it was about how we can trust God, but as they alternately sang the verses to each other, I could have sworn it was simply a love song in which the two people pledged to support and nurture each other in the face of life's pain and disappointment. "Me" was never defined as God within the song itself. A similar song, quite popular in some circles, is "He Touched Me." The melody is memorable and the message of God's healing touch is appealing, but as written it could just as easily be a romantic pop hit. Too often contemporary music uses pronouns—always masculine—alone without referents. I make it a policy not to sing any song referring to some undefined *he*. The God I know is not some vague "he," or as a young man I know explained, "Oh, you know, that guy in the sky." Again while it may be acceptable to refer to the historical Jesus as he, we should first refer to Jesus or Jesus Christ and repeat the name often enough to leave the listener with no doubt about who is being discussed. Using the male pronoun exclusively for God is theologically limiting and makes God into a gendered object.

On the other hand, a number of contemporary musicians are working diligently to write new songs and revise older hymns to be more inclusive. A number of hymnals containing revised versions of traditional hymns and newly written songs with inclusive language are becoming available. Both the *Lutheran Book of Worship* and the new Episcopal *Hymnal 1982* have sought to make their language more inclusive, and less militaristic and nationalistic, though God-language is still often masculine. The United Methodists, Presbyterians (U.S.A.), and Mennonite and Brethren churches are hard at work on revisions of their hymnals. See "Additional Resources for Worship" at the end of this book. Pastors and ministers of music would do well to supplement their own denominational hymnals with such resources. In choosing music we should always keep in mind the message of the old gospel song, " 'Whosoever' Meaneth Me."

The goal of worship, indeed the goal of the Christian faith, is to come to know God even more intimately. As we experience and understand more and more of the facets of God's nature, we are able to relate to the divine more deeply, more wholly. As we said in the beginning, the purpose of inclusive language is to find for ourselves a fuller vision, a deeper understanding of the One we love and to offer to others a relationship with the God who will heal their wounds, satisfy their longings, and make us all whole persons.


### DISCUSSION:

1. What aspect of worship is most meaningful to you?

2. In what aspect of worship do you find sexist language most offensive?

3. Choose your favorite hymn and try to revise it, using inclusive language. Then use the revision in a service to help others in the congregation see the difference.

4. How do you think your church could go about making more use of inclusive language in its worship?

# References

Baum, Gregory. *Man Becoming: God in Secular Language*. New York: Herder and Herder, 1970.

Biale, David. "The God with Breasts: El Shaddai in the Bible." *History of Religions* 21 (February 1982): 240–56.

Biles, Daniel V, III. "And Now—a Non-Sexist Bible." *Dialog* 21 (Spring 1982): 138–39.

Blackwell, Alice Stone. *Lucy Stone: Pioneer of Women's Rights*. Boston: Little, Brown, 1930.

Bloom, Anthony. *Beginning to Pray*. New York: Paulist, 1970.

Boucher, Madeleine. "Scriptural Readings: God-Language and Non-sexist Translation." *Reformed Liturgy and Music* 17 (Fall 1983): 156–59; reprinted in Withers, *Language and the Church*: Precise discussion of various titles for Jesus and their occurrence in the Synoptic Gospels.

Burbridge, Edward. *Liturgies and Offices of the Church for the Use of English Readers*. London: Bell, 1885. See pp. 334–37 for texts in Greek and Latin of the creeds of Caesarea, Nicea, Jerusalem, Constantinople, *Sacramentarium Gelasianum*, the Stowe Missal, the Mozarabic and the Roman forms.

Clark, Vivian. "Was Jesus Christ a Man's Man?" *Christianity Today*, 18 February 1983, 16–18.

Crawford, Janet, and Michael Kinnamon, eds. *In God's Image: Reflections on Identity, Human Wholeness and the Authority of Scripture*. Geneva: World Council of Churches, 1983.

Daly, Mary. *Beyond God the Father*. Boston: Beacon, 1973.

Donnelly, Dody H. *Radical Love: An Approach to Sexual Spirituality*. Minneapolis: Winston, 1984.

Edwards, James R. "Toward a Neutered Bible: Making God S/He." *Christianity Today*, 18 February 1983, 19–21. Edwards' original manuscript, titled simply "The Bible and the English Language," did not refer to "God's male gender" (article, p. 21) but raised the question "whether the masculinity of Jesus implies that God is masculine."

Evangelical Women's Caucus, International. 1357 Washington Street, West Newton, Massachusetts 02165.

Fiorenza, Elisabeth Schüssler. *In Memory of Her: A Feminist Reconstruction of Christian Origins*. New York: Crossroad, 1984.

Foster, Richard J. *Celebration of Discipline: The Path to Spiritual Growth.* San Francisco: Harper & Row, 1978.

Gordon, A. J. "The Ministry of Women." *Missionary Review of the World* 7 (December 1894): 910–21; reprinted as Gordon-Conwell Monograph #61, p. 10.

Grimke, Sarah. *Letters on the Equality of the Sexes and the Condition of Woman.* 1838 Reprint. New York: Burt Franklin, 1970.

*Guidelines for Eliminating Racism, Ageism, Handicappism and Sexism from United Methodist Resource Materials.* Dayton, Ohio: United Methodist Church General Council on Ministries, 1983.

Hamerton-Kelly, Robert. *God the Father: Theology and Patriarchy in the Teaching of Jesus.* Philadelphia: Fortress, 1979.

Hardesty, Nancy A. *Women Called to Witness: Evangelical Feminism in the Nineteenth Century.* See especially chapter 6, "Directly to the Bible." Nashville: Abingdon, 1984.

Haugerud, Joann. *The Word for Us.* Seattle, Wash.: Coalition on Women and Religion, 1977. A translation of John, Mark, Romans, and Galatians.

"He Meant What He Said: 'Him, His, He' " *Christianity Today,* 2 January 1976, 22 [354]–23 [355].

*Hearing the Word: An Inclusive-Language Liturgical Lectionary.* Washington, D.C.: St. Stephen and the Incarnation Episcopal Church, 1982.

"Inclusive Language: Do We Need It?" *Daughters of Sarah,* 11 (January/February 1985): entire issue.

Inclusive Language Lectionary Committee, Division of Education and Ministry, National Council of the Churches of Christ in the U.S.A. *An Inclusive Language Lectionary.* Philadelphia: Published for The Cooperative Publication Association by John Knox, Atlanta; Pilgrim, New York; Westminster, Philadelphia, *Readings for Year A,* 1983; *Readings for Year B,* 1984; *Readings for Year C,* 1985.

Julian of Norwich. *Showings.* Translated from the Critical Text with an Introduction by Edmund Colledge and James Walsh. New York: Paulist, 1978. This volume contains both short and long texts.

Kessel, Edward L. "A Proposed Biological Interpretation of The Virgin Birth." *Journal of the American Scientific Affiliation* 35 (September 1983): 129–36.

Keylock, Leslie R. "God Our Father *and* Mother? A bisexual nightmare from the National Council of Churches." *Christianity Today,* 11 November 1983, 50–51.

Kilpatrick, James J. "Address your prayers to God the chairperson." *Atlanta Journal and Constitution,* 23 October 1983, 3–D.

Lakoff, Robin. *Language and Woman's Place*. New York: Harper & Row, 1975.

"Letters: Neutering the Bible." *Time*, 3 December 1984, 6.

Lewis, C. S. *The Chronicles of Narnia*. 7 vols. New York: Macmillan, 1950–56.

Lutheran Church in America. *Guidelines for Avoiding Bias: For Writers and Editors*. New York: Office for Communications, Lutheran Church in America, n.d.

———. *Inclusiveness and Diversity: Gifts of God*. Philadelphia: Division of Parish Services, Lutheran Church in America, 1984. See also *Goals and Plans for Minority Ministry*, 1978.

Lyles, Jean Caffey. "The NCC's Nonsexist Lectionary." *Christian Century*, 100 (14 December 1983): 1148–50.

"Male Bias in Scripture Is High on NCC A-gender." *Christianity Today*, 2 January 1981, 58.

Marshall, Eric, and Stuart Hample. *Children's Letters to God*. New York: Essandess, 1967.

McFague, Sallie. *Metaphorical Theology: Models of God in Religious Language*. Philadelphia: Fortress, 1982.

McGraw-Hill Book Company. *Guidelines for Equal Treatment of the Sexes*. New York: McGraw-Hill, n.d.

Mickelsen, Berkeley and Alvera. "Does Male Dominance Tarnish Our Translations?" *Christianity Today*, 5 October 1979, 23–26, 29.

Micks, Marianne H. *Our Search for Identity: Humanity in the Image of God*. Philadelphia: Fortress, 1982.

Miller, Casey, and Kate Swift. *The Handbook of Nonsexist Writing: For Writers, Editors and Speakers*. New York: Barnes & Noble, a Division of Harper & Row, 1980.

———. *Words and Women: New Language in New Times*. Garden City, New York: Anchor, Anchor/Doubleday, 1977.

———. "Women and the Language of Religion." *Christian Century* 93 (14 April 1976): 353–58.

Mollenkott, Virginia Ramey. "The Bible and Linguistic Change: A feminist perspective." *The Other Side*, June 1981, 14–19.

———. *The Divine Feminine: The Biblical Image of God as Female*. New York: Crossroad, 1984.

———. "Faces of Faith: Performer in the Divine Comedy." An interview conducted by Kathleen Hayes. *The Other Side*, April/May 1985, 13–16.

———. *Speech, Silence, Action!: The Cycle of Faith*. Nashville: Abingdon, 1980. See chapters 7 and 8, "The Political Implications of Religious Imagery" and "Imaging God Inclusively."

———. *Women, Men, and the Bible*. Nashville: Abingdon Press, 1977.

Murray, Pauli. "The Holy Spirit and God Language." *The Witness* 66

(February 1983): 7–9, 19.

National Council of Teachers of English. *Guidelines for Nonsexist Use of Language*. 1976.

"NCC's Bisexual Lectionary Brings More Problems." *Christianity Today*, 16 December 1983, 40.

O'Connor, Flannery. *Three: Wise Blood, A Good Man Is Hard to Find, The Violent Bear It Away*. New York: Signet, published by New American Library, 1949, 1952, 1962, 1953, 1954, 1955, 1955, 1960, 1964, 1971, 1976, 1980.

Olson, Mark. "Comparing Two Inclusive Language Lectionaries." *Daughters of Sarah*, January/February 1985, 14–15; originally published in *The Other Side*, March 1984, 34.

Ostling, Richard N. "More Scriptures Without Sexism." *Time*, 29 October 1984, 75.

———. "O God Our [Mother and] Father: New translations seek to rid the Bible of 'male bias.'" *Time*, 24 October 1983, 56–57.

———. "Unmanning the Holy Bible." *Time*, 8 December 1980, 128.

Patterson, Ben. "The God of the NCC Lectionary Is Not the God of the Bible." *Christianity Today*, 3 February 1984, 12–13.

The Presbyterian Church in the U.S. "Language About God: A Paper Adopted by the 119th General Assembly and Commended to the Church." Atlanta: Office of the Stated Clerk of the General Assembly, Presbyterian Church in the U.S., 1980.

Ramshaw-Schmidt, Gail. "An Inclusive Language Lectionary." *Worship* 58 (January 1984): 29–36.

Rogers, Jack B. "Is God a Man?" Fuller Theological Seminary Theology, *News and Notes*, June 1975, 3–4, 18.

*The R.S.V. Interlinear Greek-English New Testament*. The Nestle Greek Text with a Literal English Translation by Alfred Marshall. Grand Rapids: Zondervan, 1958.

Ruether, Rosemary Radford. *Sexism and God-Talk: Toward a Feminist Theology*. Boston: Beacon, 1983.

Russell, Letty M., ed. *Feminist Interpretation of the Bible*. Philadelphia: Westminster, 1985.

———. ed. *The Liberating Word: A Guide to Nonsexist Interpretation of the Bible*. In cooperation with the Task Force on Sexism in the Bible, Division of Education and Ministry, National Council of the Churches of Christ in the U.S.A. Philadelphia: Westminster, 1976.

Sawicki, Marianne. *Faith and Sexism: Guidelines for Religious Educators*. New York: Crossroad, Seabury, 1979.

Sayers, Dorothy L. *Are Women Human?* Grand Rapids: Eerdmans, 1971.

Scanzoni, Letha, and Nancy A. Hardesty. *All We're Meant to Be: Biblical Feminism Today*. Revised edition. Nashville: Abingdon, 1986.

Schaef, Anne Wilson. *Women's Reality: An Emerging Female System in the White Male Society.* Minneapolis: Winston, 1981.

Spring, Beth. "A Shroud of Turin Scientist Speaks Out: Evidence that Nearly Demands a Verdict." *Christianity Today,* 7 October 1983, 58, 63–64.

Swidler, Leonard. "Jesus Was a Feminist." *Catholic World,* January 1971, 177–83.

Task Force on Language About God, Advisory Council on Discipleship and Worship, The United Presbyterian Church U.S.A. *Language About God—Opening the Door* and *The Power of Language Among the People of God.* New York: Advisory Council on Discipleship and Worship, 1020 Interchurch Center, 475 Riverside Drive, New York 10027, 1975, 1979.

Tavard, George H. "Sexist Language in Theology?" *Theological Studies* 36 (December 1975): 700–724.

Telford, John, ed. *The Letters of the Reverend John Wesley, A.M., Sometime Fellow of Lincoln College, Oxford.* 8 vols. London: Epworth, 1931.

Tennis, Diane. *Is God the Only Reliable Father?* Philadelphia: Westminster, 1985.

Tozer, A. W. *The Pursuit of God.* Harrisburg, Pennsylvania: Christian Publications, 1958.

Trible, Phyllis. *God and the Rhetoric of Sexuality.* Philadelphia: Fortress, 1978.

———. "God, Nature of, in the OT." *The Interpreter's Dictionary of the Bible.* Supplementary Volume. Nashville: Abingdon, 1976.

———. *Texts of Terror: Literary-Feminist Readings of Biblical Narratives.* Philadelphia: Fortress, 1984.

Turner, Rosa Shand. "The Increasingly Visible Female and the Need for Generic Terms." *Christian Century* 94 (16 March 1977): 248–52.

Underhill, Evelyn. *Mysticism: A Study in the Nature and Development of Man's Spiritual Consciousness,* 1911. Reprint. New York: New American Library, 1974.

Watkins, Keith. *Faithful and Fair: Transcending Sexist Language in Worship.* Nashville: Abingdon, 1981.

Watley, William D., ed. *The Word and Words: Beyond Gender in Theological and Liturgical Language.* Princeton: Women's Task Force and Worship Commission of the Consultation on Church Union, 1983.

Withers, Barbara A., ed. *Language About God in Liturgy and Scripture.* Philadelphia: Geneva, 1980.

———. *Language and the Church: Articles and Designs for Workshops.* Division of Publication Services, National Council of the Churches of Christ in the U.S.A.

# Resources for Worship

Allen, Pamela Payne. "Taking the Next Step in Inclusive Language." *The Christian Century* 103 (23 April 1986): 410–13.

Blacklock, Martha. "Popularizing Non-Sexist Liturgies." *The Witness* 64 (February 1981): 10–11.

Clark, Linda, Marian Ronan, and Eleanor Walker. *Image-Building: A Handbook for Creative Worship with Women of Christian Tradition.* New York: Pilgrim, 1981.

Community Council, Wesley Theological Seminary. *Toward More Inclusive Language in the Worship of the Church: A Position Statement.* Washington, D.C.: Wesley Theological Seminary, February 1979.

Duck, Ruth C., ed. *Bread for the Journey: Resources for Worship.* New York: Pilgrim, 1981.

———. *Flames of the Spirit: Resources for Worship.* New York: Pilgrim, 1985.

Hammack, Mary L. *A Dictionary of Women in Church History.* Chicago: Moody, 1984.

Neufer Emswiler, Thomas and Sharon. *Wholeness in Worship.* San Francisco: Harper & Row, 1980.

———. *Women and Worship: A Guide to Nonsexist Hymns, Prayers, and Liturgies.* 2d ed. New York: Harper & Row, 1984.

Swidler, Arlene, ed. *Sistercelebrations: Nine Worship Experiences.* Philadelphia: Fortress, 1974.

Task Force on Language Guidelines. *Words That Hurt, Words That Heal: Language About God and People.* A churchwide study from the 1984 General Conference of the United Methodist Church. Nashville: Graded Press, 1985.

Walrath, Douglas Alan. *Leading Churches Through Change.* Nashville: Abingdon, 1979.

White, James F. "The Words of Worship: Beyond Liturgical Sexism." *The Christian Century* 95 (13 December 1978): 1202–06.

*Worship* 52 (November 1978): entire issue.

## Prayer:

The Episcopal Church. *The Book of Common Prayer.* New York: Church Hymnal Corporation and Seabury, 1979.

Hamman, A., ed. *Early Christian Prayers.* Trans. Walter Mitchell. Chicago: Henry Regnery, 1961.

Kirk, James G. *When We Gather: A Book of Prayers for Worship.* Philadelphia: Geneva, Year A, 1983; Year B, 1984; Year C, 1985.

## Proclamation:

Deen, Edith. *Great Women of the Christian Faith*. New York: Harper & Brothers, 1959.

Hardesty, Nancy A. *Great Women of Faith*. Grand Rapids: Baker, 1980; paperback, Nashville: Abingdon, 1982.

Mason, Maggie. *Women Like Us: Learn More About Yourself through Studies of Bible Women*. Waco, Texas: Word, 1978.

Moltmann-Wendel, Elisabeth. *The Women Around Jesus*. New York: Crossroad, 1982.

Otwell, John H. *And Sara Laughed: The Status of Women in the Old Testament*. Philadelphia: Westminster, 1977.

Stagg, Evelyn, and Frank Stagg. *Women in the World of Jesus*. Philadelphia: Westminster, 1978.

Wahlberg, Rachel Conrad. *Jesus According to a Woman*. New York: Paulist, 1975.

———. *Jesus and the Freed Woman*. New York: Paulist, 1978.

## Hymns:

Duck, Ruth C., and Michael G. Bausch, eds. *Everflowing Streams: Songs for Worship*. New York: Pilgrim, 1981.

The Ecumenical Women's Center, ed. *Because We Are One People: Songs for Worship*. Chicago: Ecumenical Women's Center, 1974. Available from Ecumenical Women's Center, 1653 West School Street, Chicago, Illinois 60657.

The Episcopal Church, *The Hymnal 1982*. New York: Church Hymnal Corporation for the Church Pension Fund, 1985.

Huber, Jane Parker. *Joy in Singing*. Atlanta: The Office of Women and the Joint Office of Worship of the Presbyterian Church (U.S.A.), 1983.

Lodge, Ann, ed. *Creation Sings*. Philadelphia: Westminster, 1980.

Lutheran Church in America, et al. *Lutheran Book of Worship*. Minneapolis: Augsburg; Philadelphia: Board of Publication, Lutheran Church in America, 1978. Compilers of this volume have made a considered effort in the direction of inclusive language.

Neufer Emswiler, Sharon and Thomas, eds. *Put on Your Party Clothes*. Normal, Illinois: Wesley Foundation, 1977.

———. *Sisters and Brothers, Sing!* Normal, Illinois: Wesley Foundation, 1977.

Rose, Steve. *A New Hymnal*. Stockbridge, Massachusetts: Persephone Music, 1980.

Wren, Brian. *Faith Looking Forward: The Hymns and Songs of Brian Wren*. Carol Stream, Illinois: Hope, 1983.

———. *Praising a Mystery*. Carol Stream, Illinois: Hope, 1986.

# Subject Index

# Scripture Index

**Gen.**

| | |
|---|---|
| 1:2 | 54 |
| 1:26– | 8, 19–20 |
| 28 | |
| 2:4–23 | 81 |
| 2:4–3:24 | 21 |
| 3:16 | 73 |
| 14:19, 22 | 22 |
| 15:1 | 37 |
| 16:13 | 22 |
| 17:1, 5–6 | 23 |
| 18:25 | 33 |
| 20:1–18 | 25 |
| 21:33 | 21 |
| 22:8 | 21 |
| 25:23 | 26 |
| 28:3 | 23 |
| 29:4–12 | 33 |
| 29:31–35 | 25 |
| 30:22 | 35 |
| 35:11 | 23 |
| 43:14 | 23 |
| 48:3–4 | 23 |
| 49:9 | 35 |
| 49:25–26 | 23 |

**Exod.**

| | |
|---|---|
| 3:2 | 38 |
| 3:14–15 | 20–21 |
| 13:21 | 37, 54 |
| 15:16 | 21 |
| 17:15 | 21 |
| 19:4 | 34 |
| 20:4 | 10 |
| 20:7 | 29 |
| 31:3 | 54 |
| 33:19 | 25 |
| 34:6 | 25 |

**Num.**

| | |
|---|---|
| 11:12 | 36 |
| 24:17 | 38 |

**Deut.**

| | |
|---|---|
| 4:31 | 25 |
| 5:9 | 19 |
| 32 | 36 |
| 32:6 | 23 |
| 32:11 | 34 |
| 32:15, 18 | 20 |
| 32:18 | 23 |
| 33:26 | 38 |
| 33:29 | 37 |

**Judg.**

| | |
|---|---|
| 3:10 | 54 |
| 5:3 | 21 |
| 6:24 | 21 |
| 9:46 | 22 |
| 14:6 | 54 |

**Ruth**

| | |
|---|---|
| 1:20–21 | 26 |

**1 Sam.**

| | |
|---|---|
| 1:1–10 | 25 |
| 1:26–27 | 11 |
| 2:2 | 36 |
| 15:29 | 22 |
| 17:26, 36 | 38 |
| 24:3 | 76 |

**2 Sam.**

| | |
|---|---|
| 22:2–3 | 36–37 |
| 22:32 | 36–37 |
| 22:47 | 36–37 |

**1 Kings**

| | |
|---|---|
| 3:21 | 77 |
| 18 | 11, 38 |

**2 Chron.**

| | |
|---|---|
| 30:9 | 25 |

**Neh.**

| | |
|---|---|
| 9:17 | 20, 25 |

**Job**

| | |
|---|---|
| 3:1–26 | 25 |
| 10:10–11 | 33 |
| 10:18–19 | 25, 32 |
| 31:13–15 | 25 |
| 39:27–30 | 34 |

**Ps.**

| | |
|---|---|
| 3:3 | 37 |
| 18:2 | 36 |
| 18:31 | 20 |
| 22:9–10 | 25 |
| 23 | 11, 33 |
| 27:1 | 37 |
| 28:7 | 37 |
| 31:2–3 | 36 |
| 33 | 38 |
| 33:20 | 37 |
| 42:2 | 38 |
| 43:4 | 14 |
| 44:1–2 | 59–60 |
| 50:22 | 20 |
| 59:11 | 37 |
| 62:2, 6 | 36 |
| 68:4 | 38 |
| 68:11 | 78 |
| 71:3 | 36 |
| 71:6 | 26 |
| 84:9 | 37 |
| 86:15 | 25 |
| 91:1–2, 4 | 36 |
| 103:8 | 25 |
| 103:13 | 26 |
| 111:4 | 25 |
| 112:4 | 25 |
| 114:2 | 37 |
| 114:7 | 20 |
| 115:9, 10, 11 | 37 |
| 119:114 | 37 |
| 131:2 | 24 |
| 139:19 | 20 |
| 144:2 | 36 |
| 145:8 | 25 |